TIMES
SQUARE

For Trisha

TIMES
SQUARE

Text © Brendan Glacken 1994.
Cover Design Wendy Shea.

First Published November 1994.
by Irish Times Books.
10-16 D'Olier Street, Dublin.

ISBN 0 907011 22 5

Distribution: Irish Times General Services.
Telephone: (01) 679 2022 Ext. 309. Fax: (01) 679 7991.
Printed in Republic of Ireland by Colour Books Ltd.

CONTENTS

LIVING WITH THE CHRISTMAS LEFTOVERS

Around this time of year, households all over the country will already be wondering what to do with the Christmas leftovers. But never fear: just follow our guidelines and all will be well.

Leftover Guest. This will usually be a distant male relation of middle age who arrived on Christmas Eve, having drink on him but not with him, and citing an invitation to which no one will now confess. He is now stuck limpet-like in your home, is rarely out of range of your liquor cabinet, and you have discovered his return ticket is open-ended. What to do? Firstly, even in desperation, do not makes jokes to him about moving in his furniture, or any similar remarks. This man thinks irony is some kind of hard ornamental material and is quite likely to be on the phone to a removal service within the hour. You could begin a slow whispering campaign about a rare tropical disease creeping through your family, or a curse handed down through the generations, or the incipient, lethal mania of your spouse. If nothing else works you will just have to shoot the so-and-so. Do not worry too much about the consequences: Supreme Court judges are human too, and at their age are quite likely to have had a similar experience.

Leftover Plans for a Quiet Christmas. Just throw them right out. Get an identical new set at the same time next year.

Leftover nervous system. Unlike the turkey, there will hardly be much of this remaining, so it will not present serious problems. Carefully gather up the flitters, shreds or tatters to which your system has been reduced, and lay them in a quiet room. Draw the curtains and remove all sources of noise. Decline all offers of assistance from anyone under 12. Given time and a peaceful environment your nerves will reconstitute themselves into a system which should be re-usable within six months.

Leftover Carol Singers. The uses to which seasonal superfluities can be put are rather limited. If a good snowfall has occurred anywhere near you, you could bury them in it for a week with their arms outstretched: when disinterred, they will make perfectly serviceable coat-stands.

Leftover Christmas Declarations. As the year draws to a close, all sorts of glittering declarations, gaudy promises and assurances will have been made (in good faith, though not good sense) regarding one's behaviour, drinking patterns, work habits, DIY ambitions, self-improvement plans etc. With Christmas over, however, these declarations will inevitably lose their glitter and may indeed be compared by unkinder family members to the Christmas tree adornments, namely a load of (coloured) balls. Never mind. Take all your declarations down and pack them away carefully: when you take them

9

out again next year, just dust them off and they will be as good as new.

The 300-odd Shopping Days Left Over Until Next Christmas. Lie down in a darkened room and try not to think about them. Repeat softly to yourself the soothing mantra, *Christmas is over, Christmas is over.*

Leftover Pet. This will be the kitten or puppy presented to a smaller member of your family by a family friend, now a family ex-friend. Your child has played with it for precisely seventeen minutes over five days, and by now its droppings (the pet's, not the child's), which are in inverse proportion to its size, have adorned every single carpet in the house. You have tripped on the creature seven times and stood on it eleven times, only five of them deliberately. The thing has a soprano squeal and a python-like bite and demonstrates both regularly.

What is to be done? If you are concomitantly stuck with *Leftover Guest* (see above) you could try training the so-called pet as an organic assault unit; leave the door open and one committed attack might then see off two leftover problems. Otherwise invite the ex-friend to babysit the child and the animal and just disappear for a few weeks.

Leftover Christmas Dreams. Let them fade away quietly of their own accord. Have no regrets. They will return, as they always do, next Christmas, just as beautiful as they always were, and always will be.

TIME, GENTLEMEN, PLEASE!

At this time of year you may well be thinking, and perhaps not too positively, about the passage of time itself. You are possibly beginning to think you have no control over it. Well, not so: at least, apparently, not for the US Commerce Department. In a covert little notice in this paper not long ago, the Department revealed that from the end of last June, a leap second was being added to world time, in order "to match the super-accurate atomic time and keep it in step with the Earth's rotation." This correction was necessary, we were blithely informed, because the Earth is "a poor clock compared with modern atomic clocks."

This "news" item was slipped into the weather report, sandwiched between Outlook ("mostly sunny again, but rain possibly later in the extreme west") and the Blood Transfusion Service details ("Mobile units at Mullingar and Navan"). No further information was advanced. Not another word. So what on earth – no pun intended – does it all mean? Well, for it start it would appear one's life expectancy is officially increased (though you may first have to take out US citizenship). If you have just been born, and are hopeful of surviving for, say, 80 years, you should now be able to bank on a further 20 leap year seconds. If, at the close of your 80 years, this period fails to materialise, and you pop off prematurely, hitherto having been in reasonable health, your surviving relatives should consider suing the US Commerce Department. The way I see it, they *owe* you.

Philosophers make a big thing of time, mostly because philosophers tend to have a lot of it on their hands. Yet lots of them would probably try to tell you that 20 extra seconds are neither here nor there. So what you say if you meet one of those fellows is – wouldn't you rather be here than there? If only for another 20 seconds? (And don't let them answer back, unless you have 15 or 20 hours to spare, which would in itself negate the main thrust of your argument). Looking at the other end of the health-and-fitness spectrum, even if you were lying on your deathbed you could still feasibly write "null and void" across your will, sign it – and rescind your decision again, all in less than 20 seconds. Even at death's door you might still be able to pick up your pen and, within the same supposedly negligible time period, scrawl across your final testament "Families are death: I leave every last penny to my mistress Veronique." Such a flourish would certainly ensure the testing of time's overblown reputation as the great healer.

And what is one to make of the US Commerce Department's boastful assertion that the Earth is a poor clock "compared with modern atomic clocks"? The Earth and its movements have, in terms of time-keeping over the years, provided perfect satisfaction for many millions of people, possibly even those for whom the Earth has *never* moved. Many more people will sympathise with the attitude that anything after the sundial was a waste of time (so to speak) and, aesthetically, a retrograde step.

This whole business of a supposed need for ultra-accurate time-keeping has got completely out of hand, or at any rate wrist, and where has it got us? Today's typical timepiece is a nauseating throwaway affair, usually in lurid neon or aggressive black, and packed with foolish functions allowing you to tell the time in countries you would not dream of visiting, gauge your instep measurement to a tenth of a millimetre and calculate the mean average rainfall in the Fiji Islands over the past 15 years. On the rare occasion when one of these function-filled monstrosities is consulted simply for the time of day, it inevitably drops dead of battery failure.

Now, just when one has begun to come to terms with horrible digital clocks and sleep buttons and ugly LED read-out and even clocks that wake you up with an American-accented voice synthesizer, one is expected to appreciated the added "advantages", whatever they may be, of atomic clocks.

I say: bring back the good old no-nonsense alarm clock, the one with a winder at the back, a little knob to turn to hour and second hands, another to set the alarm, a couple of great big silver bells on top and a button on the side which you whack when the alarm goes off. They come in simple primary colours, their only pretence to sophistication is a luminous painted dial and they don't need batteries. So what if they miss out on a leap second here and there? As for the US Commerce Department, what can one say to them but time, gentlemen, please?

THERE'S NO SUCH THING AS A FREE LAUNCH

The latter part of 1992 saw a rash of travel "giveaway" offers on various retail products.

I write this cautionary tale aboard a jet airliner on my way, along with 200 other unhappy passengers, to a destination which none of us can remember. Indeed none of us cares, because our only wish is to go home. But that is out of the question. For as you may guess, we are all victims of the Great Retail Travel Giveaway.

This sinister marketing operation began innocently enough in the pre-Christmas period with consumers being offered, on a variety of goods, cut-price flights to selected destinations. Why anyone should imagine that a person purchasing a new washing machine might simultaneously harbour a desire to visit New York on the cheap remains a mystery, but the success of the promotion was unprecedented. And before long, cut-price, and eventually free, travel all over the world was being offered with just about every imaginable consumer commodity.

The result is that at any given time, entire communities, amounting to a not inconsiderable section of the Irish population, are crowding trains and aeroplanes as they "avail" of the "opportunities" to visit places they hithero did not care about, had often never heard of, and of which they have quickly become heartily sick. My own experience is salutary. It began the day I went out to buy an ordinary toaster. Unfortunately the thing carried a Special Offer – which I was not quick enough to spot – of a train ticket to Limerick. As it happens I have never had the slightest desire to visit Limerick, by train or any other means, but it was too late: a ridiculously pleased manager insisted on escorting me to the station right away and bundling me on to a first-class carriage.

On alighting from the train in Limerick I had to revive myself with a double brandy. I wondered why the barman looked so delighted, and soon I felt a dreadful chill dissipating the heat of the liquor. Sure enough, it transpired my simple purchase "entitled" me to a flight to New York. I begged, I pleaded, I invented a Mafia hitman waiting for me in Manhattan, all to no avail. The lunatic insisted on driving me straightaway to Shannon.

By the time I arrived in Kennedy Airport I was of course thoroughly confused and, thinking a sugar boost might help, I decided to buy a bar of chocolate. In my upset state I failed to see the manic glint in the saleslady's eye, and to my horror, when I undid the wrapper I found I had now fallen in for a trip for two to Paris, or Rome, or Amsterdam – I can't remember. The travel giveaway madness had crossed the Atlantic! But the saleslady was ludicrously pleased. I broke down, and stuttered through my tears that I was on my own and just wanted to go home. It was all in vain. Laughing gaily at my naivety, she immediately produced from under the counter a travelling companion kept by the firm for just such an emergency.

As it turned out, I was at least able to swop free travel horror stories with Martha (that was her name) on our way to wherever we were going. Her own consumer history was lengthy and pitiful, involving as it did a great deal of new kitchen equipment and Flexi-break vouchers, all of which launched the poor woman on the slippery slope, which of course turned out to be a runway.

Still, there is hope on the horizon (not that much horizon is visible up here). The passengers with whom I am currently travelling are getting very excited about an inboard promotion now under way. Indeed some of them got so excited initially, at the idea of yet another travel promotion, that they rushed for the emergency exits and seven were lost, poor souls, because after all we *are* flying at 20,000 feet above sea level. Anyway, it seems all we have to do is to accept, *gratis,* a duty-free bottle of this new liqueur to put us in line for a unique offer: we will be escorted home, or to any marketing-free zone of our choice, for a full fortnight. And here's the real treat: the sponsors give an unequivocal guarantee that no travel concessions are included.

There are a few of us, however, who have been driven, or rather flown, to such lengths that we remain suspicious. Who knows but that when the last drop is drained from the bottle, there will materialise on the back of the label that most terrifying promotional promise: "Congratulations! This empty bottle entitles you to a round trip to..." Only then will the poor tortured and travel-weary consumer realise the truth of the old adage that there is no such thing as a free launch.

DON'T BE COWED BY THE BEEF TRIBUNAL

The long-running investigation into the meat processing business, otherwise known as the Beef Tribunal, resumed in January 1993.

Now that the Beef Tribunal has resumed, and with the principal players having already given their evidence, it is only a matter of time before every man, woman and child in the country is called on to contribute their tuppenceworth from the dock. This is one of the advantages of democracy. But are you prepared? This is your big chance to make a national impact – or to make a complete fool of yourself.

However, merely by following our simple advice, you can be sure of achieving distinction in the dock.

Dress. Follow the three "C"s – clean, comfortable and casual. But under no circumstances should you wear a suit. Your solicitor, your senior counsel, the State solicitor and State senior counsel, all of the junior counsels, the devils, the stenographers, the court attendants, the gofers and anyone else present with even the most tenuous of links to the legal profession will undoubtedly be sporting more expensive suits, and you will accordingly be at an immediate sartorial and psychological disadvantage. The only advantage in your wearing a suit in these circumstances lies in the certainty of not being mistaken for a member of the media.

Demeanour. All-important, this. You must look confident, but not more so than the Justice. You may even look cocky, but not more so than the Senior Counsels. Smile at your peril, except when your are utterly stymied, i.e. caught out. If you feel confused you may well have good reason to, but take care to avoid actually *looking* confused. Thoughtful nodding while a barrister makes an utterly incomprehensible point will add to your standing.

Giving Evidence. If asked about your diary, as you certainly will be, and about certain entries on certain days, on no account should you read aloud foolish nerd-like excerpts such as "Mary's birthday. Buy flowers on way home" unless you wish to lose all street credibility. The Tribunal is not interested in such indications of a pathetic little semi-detached suburban existence, and neither is the public. So make some image-boosting back-entries now. Insert a few gnomic references to "CJ" and/or "LG" which will vaguely impress without actually incriminating. But for God's sake be careful. And if it *is* Mary's birthday, the only way you can retrieve the situation (brilliantly, indeed) is by remarking, as if it should be obvious to all, that the reference is to the President.

On the other hand, you will gain rather than lose standing if your wife's name is Ann.

Cross-examination. You will recall the Thurber cartoon in which the cross-examing barrister produces a kangaroo from behind his back, holds it aloft by the ears in front of the shocked defendant and declaims triumphantly, "Perhaps *this* will refresh your memory !" Be prepared for this sort of surprise attack. Check that your diary is free of kangaroo entries, or similar. Resist the temptation to make jokes about kangaroo courts. The judiciary has a sense of humour (there are at least two precedents for judges laughing aloud in court over the past 40 years) but it is comprehensible only to its members.

Barrister techniques. It is a well-known fact that barristers have no emotions of any kind; if any remain by the time training is completed, they are surgically removed in a specially-equipped operating theatre in King's Inns. Accordingly if a barrister at any time rounds on you in what looks like anger, or pleasure, or surprise, take no notice. These exhibitions are *not* emotions, merely weapons in the professional armoury, and are effective only if they elicit a visible or audible reaction. Therefore all you have to do is look blank and keep quiet.

Rhetorical flourishes. If you have nothing else to say, fire off a burst of poetry. Anything vaguely rhetorical will do: it really depends on what image you wish to get across. Quote Seamus Heaney, and you inadvertently align yourself with the Establishment, which may not necessarily be to your advantage. Quote Brendan Kennelly and the charm may backfire – and you may alienate important people who attended UCD. Choose Patrick Kavanagh and you become an honest rural figure ruined by the sophisticated city. Given the circumstances of the Beef Tribunal and its most prominent figures, Kavanagh is strongly recommended.

COUNSELLING: THE HIDDEN ADDICTION

Strong public concern has been expressed at recent revelations concerning the unprecedented growth over the past few years in counselling, described by one commentator as "the hidden addiction". The number of registered counsellors in Ireland has now apparently risen to over 100,000, but this is only the tip of the iceberg, as, unofficially, it is estimated the real figure is closer to 300,000. The fear now is that it will not be long before the number of counsellors exceeds those being counselled.

Certainly one does not have to travel far, particularly in the capital city, to find evidence of the extent of the counselling epidemic. Discarded self-help leaflets litter the streets, helpline numbers are scribbled in every phone booth, even reputable newspapers carry advertisements for counsellors desperate to feed their insidious habit.

One of the problems is that most counsellors look like normal people: there is nothing on the surface to indicate their true nature. Most of them are reassuringly middle-class, well-dressed and well-spoken, but they are quite blatant about their proclivities: if you ask them what they do, most will shamelessly admit to being counsellors.

Nevertheless, it seems unfair to treat counsellors as pariahs. Many of them deserve only sympathy: indeed the results of a recent sample of 300 counsellors showed that 213 had themselves been counselled in their own impressionable years.

We talked to a self-confessed counsellor about how his habit developed. Joe (not his real name) said: "It all began when I was in my early twenties. I got into the habit of giving well-intentioned advice on everything from DIY to love matters to my friends and colleagues. Before long I was actively seeking situations where I could indulge my vice, meetings, pub gatherings, whist drives, anywhere I could find people with problems. Even if they didn't have problems I was able to convince them they had. But this wasn't enough for me. To feed my addiction, I set up my own therapy centre where I now counsel about fifty clients a week, most of them with no identifiable problems of any kind. I just can't seem to stop."

To counter the explosion in counselling, one suggestion is that the Government should consider providing free clients recruited from the ranks of the unemployed. This would at least help keep some counsellors off the streets, as well as the broadcasting and print media.

If the growth in counselling is allowed to continue at the present rate, the worry is that violence could erupt as out-of-control hordes of counsellors compete viciously for a dwindling pool of clients. Already there have been numerous incidents around Dublin's Fitzwilliam Square – a notorious no-go area where counselling is rife – with ordinary people being solicited by counsellors desperate to feed their habit.

We talked to one of these victims about her recent terrifying experience in Upper Fitzwilliam Street. Assumpta Higgins, a lady in her early fifties, was on her way last Monday morning to her cleaning job in the ESB headquarters when she was approached by a well-dressed man of about 35.

"Straight up, he asks me did I need any counselling. For what? I asked him politely. You have to be careful not to upset these people. He says, 'well surely you've got some problems.' What kind of problems? I said, laughing. That was a mistake, I know now. These people are dreadfully serious, you see. 'Well *you* know', he says, 'emotional problems, sexual difficulties, problems *relating* to people, that sort of thing.'

"Well, I told him straight off I had no problems at all. I *have* a few problems with my relations, especially my husband's mother, but that's none of his business, is it? I just wanted to get rid of him, you see. Then *he* says, 'If you think you haven't any problems, then you certainly *have* a problem. And I want to help you.'

"I got frightened then, I don't mind admitting. I don't know about you, but I run a mile when someone says they can help me. Luckily, this other fellow came along then, wearing a nice double-breasted suit, and ever so politely *he* says, 'What seems to be the problem?' Straightaway I knew he was one of them, too. And the *other* fellow says, real aggressive like, 'I'm looking after *her* problem, what's *yours*?' Next thing I know, they were trying to counsel each other, and arguing about whose clinic they should go back to. So I ran, just left them to it. The Government should definitely do something. A mind isn't safe on the street these days."

BOOK YOUR VALENTINE'S VISITOR NOW

Well, here it comes again. Yes, less than a week to go to St Valentine's Day, and once more you are faced with the annual difficulty of appearing warm, witty, thoughtful, considerate, loving, caring, passionately committed and sexually charged, while simultaneously having full regard for harassment strictures and political correctness guidelines. All this within the confines of a folded piece of thin card! What's more, the object of your affections probably expects you to be original, and wasn't greatly impressed by your efforts last year. So what's to be done?

Have no fears. *Valentine's Visitors* are here to help. Times have changed, and no one can be satisfied these days with the dreary exchange of cards, chocolates and teddy bears. Women want more. So do men, if it comes to that. And we at *Valentine's Visitors* are here to give it to them, on your behalf. We have a wide range of professional services, some of which are listed below, and all very reasonably priced. All you have to do is choose, and leave the rest to us.

The Serenade Service. A great favourite with our customers last year, this involves a specially chosen staff member (see our colour catalogue) visiting your Valentine's home late at night and warbling seductively on your behalf under his/her balcony (balconies supplied and fitted on request). Should the serenade prove particularly stimulating (your loved one should be so lucky) the use of an extending aluminium ladder is also included, though a small personal insurance surcharge will be incurred for high-rise apartment blocks.

The Deluxe Service. This includes all the traditional gifts of the day, i.e. card (swollen silk-padded heart motif optional), chocolates, teddy, silk underwear, etc., all hand-delivered by one of our devilishly-attractive staff, who are further briefed to whisper selected sweet nothings in your beloved's ear (where else, sez you). Our Valentine's Visitor will sit for as long as you specify with the object of your affections, sharing the chocolates, the champagne and, if required, the silk underwear, while simultaneously wittering on about the wonder of love, the moon, the sea, the stars, the way his/her eyes catch the light, and all sorts of other romantic drivel appropriate to the day. Merely tick your requirements and let us do the rest.

Stud Service. You want something, let's be honest, a bit raunchier. Fine. Why should you be embarrassed to say so? Even old St Valentine himself, Patron Saint of Coyness though he be, must have felt some stirrings down there now and again. Right? So let us recommend our *Valentine's Visitor* Stud Service. No piddling about here with wimpy chocolates and teddy bears! No: our staff are trained to make love professionally on your behalf in a wide variety of positions as approved in all reputable sex manuals. Just mark the number (the position number, that is) on the enclosed service menu and we will look after the rest. Whatever you select, your Valentine is guaranteed satisfaction on a no-quibble basis – though we can't guarantee "no-nibble", ha-ha!

Note: for more specialised services, check out your sealed blue folder.

Budget Special Service. A bit short of the readies? Never mind: just choose from our "Nice Price" selection. No fancy chocolates or silk underwear here, obviously – but you can still get your card, your chocolate bar and your three-pack of cotton unisex panties all personally delivered on the day. The cost? Only a tenner. It's a cheapo, we're not denying it, but if your Valentine is dumb enough to believe it's the thought that counts, this will still do the trick.

Surprise Service. Still can't decide? Then why not go for our Mystery Package? Obviously we can't reveal the exact contents of this little box of goodies – but suffice it to say your Valentine will not be disappointed. We *can* tell you there's something naughty in *crepe-de-chine* in there – plus another little something powered by four R6 batteries! The Mystery Package doesn't come cheap, but believe us, it's worth it, if only for the look on your Valentine's face.

PUBLICANS STAR IN THE CRYING GAME

With Budget Day looming, the vintners – publicans in their Sunday suits – have again been rallying customers to their worthy cause, namely the defence of drink from further tax increases. Heartrending pleas have gone out about the pressures on the "dependent families" in the beleaguered trade, the high costs of pint-pulling, the pathetically low profit margins, the threat to the tourist industry and the need to *reduce* tax in order to increase revenue to the Exchequer. And yet there are probably still people out there who think publicans don't care about the national coffers.

This year, the publicans have highlighted the "plight" of the rural pub, where attendance and consumption have apparently been cut back by the police applying petty and mean-minded laws on drink-driving, with the risible intention of reducing carnage on the roads.

The typical Irish rural pub is, as everybody knows, the repository of all things glorious in Ireland's heritage. It is a centre – almost, one might say, an interpretive centre, of age-old tradition, chat, anecdote, music, history, philosophy and *craic;* the availability of alcohol being only a diversionary sideline, a mere incidental. Indeed the rural pub is clearly the next best thing to a charitable enterprise; so obviously we should look after it, and after the people who so selflessly run it.

Accordingly, the publicans will be glad to hear the details – leaked by a sympathetic TD – of a private Dáil debate on this supreme crisis facing the country. Appropriately enough, the special debate got under way after closing time in the Dáil bar late last night. It began with an impassioned address by the guest speaker, well-known conservationist and documentary-maker of Gargle Valley, Bray, who has made a series of award-winning films about the rural Irish publican, his habits and habitat. According to him, it is only a decade or so since *Publicanus Rusticanus* was a thriving countryside species, to be encountered on almost every road and even boreen at any time, day or night. The film-maker then went on to paint a heart-rending picture of how this lovable creature – most typically a gentle, plump, florid-faced specimen, jovial by nature and genial by training – had slowly been worn down, and was now a threatened species with many of the threats coming, quite disgracefully, from a Government minion, namely the Collector General.

He went on to describe the wholesale destruction of the habitat of *Publicanus Rusticanus*, usually a warm, womblike structure which by its nature drew in other country species like *Layaboutus Localis,* and occasionally even more exotic visitors such as *Touristus Gullibilis.* This rich rural community life was now rapidly disappearing, and we were the poorer as a nation.

Environmentalist John Green TD picked up on the habitat theme, spelling out the tragic losses in terms of local rural beauty. Gone for ever, he averred, was the inviting expanse of the concrete gable end of the typical country pub; gone from inside it were the irreplaceable beauty-board and the historically-stained velour seating with its original springs. We were witnessing the passing of great glories: "Ni fheicfidh a leithéid ann arís."

Warming to his theme, Green eloquently mourned the passing of the giant, haunting neon lights that adorned the typical rural pub, beaming across huge swathes of countryside their promise of light and joy within. Lying forlorn too were the majestic gravel-strewn car parks with which selfless rural publicans had replaced useless fields. Destined to fade from the folk memory forever were venerable, patterned, multi-stained carpets, vintage flock wallpaper, tobacco-stained ceilings and processed cheese sandwiches: the overall loss to the nation was incalculable.

Green sat down to huge applause, and other speakers took up the now familiar tale of fading pub glories. Rural Interpretive Expert Joe Peat TD drew attention to the superb Tannoy systems with which many selfless rural publicans had bedecked their premises, the louder and better to inform customers when it was time to get the hell out: the publican's only consideration being to dispatch the happy customers home to their loved ones as quickly as possible.

Another TD drew attention to the generous charity service of many publicans in allowing some poor lonely souls remain on the premises after closing time despite the threat to their own licences. And who, asked another, could possibly begrudge simple rural publicans the second jobs they were often obliged to accept, sometimes even in the Dáil itself? Everyone knew their concerns were for their country, the tourism trade, the national heritage, the Exchequer, the unemployed, the hungry and the thirsty; but rarely, if ever, for themselves.

It was all enough to make a grown man cry into his pint; if, following next Wednesday's Budget, he could ever afford a pint again.

IT MAY BE LENT, BUT YOU'LL GET IT BACK

So it's Lent. And all around you, people have just "given up", in no particular order of precedence or combination, drink, cigarettes, red meat, sweets, overspending, late nights, swearing at the children, kicking the dog, cheating on partners, fiddling expenses, avoiding housework, evading tax, insulting the boss, faking sick leave, mocking the mother-in-law, and so on.

You, on the other hand, have given up precisely nothing. And you are thinking to yourself, bitterly, what are these people, crazy? See themselves as some sort of saints, or what? Got the notion that penitence – dammit, the rest of us think that's the name of a painkiller – is going to help? Wasn't the Budget enough for these people? This is 1993, come on !

You carry on with your unspoken diatribe – we know your game, you want to make the rest of us feel guilty, greedy and gutless. Worse, your so-called penitence isn't even for yourself alone. No, you're doing it partly for *us*. Well thanks a *mil*, suckers. You're welcome. Be our guests. You want help with your stash of booze and ciggies? We'll take it off your hands. Be our moral Atlas, take it all on those upright shoulders, and just keep out of our *sight*.

But you are wrong, you know, in your unspoken rage. Misguided. Quite mistaken. Because Lent is a much misunderstood season. We have all heard of the Irishman who, invited up for a drink by Mae West, declined on account of it being Lent. She then suggested he call when he got it back – and he's probably *still* confused. But much has changed. And the new thinking is that Lent is something not to be endured, but to be enjoyed. This is a feelgood age, and not even Lent is unaffected: a specially-commissioned survey now throws light on the new outlook.

Our first interviewee, a lady, told of her novel idea of giving up her husband for Lent. She was delighted with the way things were working out. "This way", she explained, "you get penitence for two people, and to tell you the truth, there isn't much pain involved for me." She amusingly pointed out that while half the business of giving up something for Lent was, as she understood it, to forego pleasure in order to assuage guilt, she was now feeling guilty because she wasn't feeling pain. On the other hand, her husband was making up for her: he was feeling pain and felt she should feel guilty! She couldn't get over what fun the whole thing was. Nobody had ever properly explained Lent to her before.

A husband who had followed a similar course – giving up his wife for Lent – was, however, not so happy. Pressed on his difficulties, he admitted his wife hadn't noticed. But surely the point was to deny *himself* something?

Exactly, he said, but he just didn't like the way she was reacting. Or rather, not reacting. And had he tried telling her he had given her up? Yes. That had made things worse. In what way? She had started *laughing*. Not only that, but she had said, why give her up just for Lent? Why not carry on? He was confused. But wasn't he glad to have her approval? Wasn't that good in itself?

Well, maybe. Another man had given up all of his self-improvement courses, and his self had felt an immediate improvement. There was something new to be learnt in this, he felt, though he agreed that attempting to learn something new was what had brought him to his original predicament.

A particularly sensitive New Man had given up crying, quiche-eating, babysitting and counselling. He felt better, but worried, since he was supposed to feel worse, yet happy that he was worried because he didn't feel as bad as he thought he should. As a New Man he had long ago learned not to feel guilty, yet now he felt he might have forgotten the distinction between innocence and guilt, which made him feel just a weeny bit guilty, which may or not have been a step in the right direction. "God, it's all so complicated, so is God, come to think of it and of course so is life, so maybe that's all right."

We left him to talk to our final interviewee. Had he given up anything? Yes. Given up what? "Nothing. Just given up." It dawned on us, and we duly put it to him, that this was the ultimate indulgence. He was taken aback, but forced to agree. Would he or would he not take it up again when Lent came to an end? He thought hard about this and then answered "I give up." It wasn't a riddle, we explained politely. But he insisted it was.

RTE TO FILM A YEAR IN THE PROVINCES

Peter Mayle's A Year in Provence, his story of moving to France, became a best-seller.

It can now be exclusively revealed that A *Year in the Provinces,* Peter Wayle's bestselling account of his move to rural Ireland and the idyllic life he found there, has been bought by RTE for a six-figure sum and is to be filmed in 104 hour-long episodes for screening on a twice-weekly basis over the coming year.

At this stage, there can be few people who have not heard of Peter Wayle's remarkable book, an enthralling account of how he and his wife Annie, having thrown up successful and well-paid careers in Dublin, set out to live more simple and fulfilling lives in Ireland's unspoiled countryside.

Having spent their first three months staying in bed-and-breakfast accommodation all over Ireland – Peter's chapter on B&B breakfast crockery is a valuable social document in itself – the Wayles settled in a picturesque old farmhouse near the tiny village of Ballybyug in the rolling countryside three miles outside Belmullet, choosing the site for its enchanting view of a unique historic monument – which locals regarded with comical disrespect (one of them describing it, in Peter Wayle's hilarious quote, as "just an oul' handball alley").

Things were refreshingly different in Ballybyug. On the very first day, Annie went along to the local store and, in her own words – "I discovered the sliced pan." She was enchanted. "The wonderful thing was the lack of choice. It was a liberation." Peter agreed enthusiastically. "Back in Dublin, you felt a complete fool if you couldn't specify in detail exactly what kind of bread you wanted – and *why.* You had to sort through sourdough bread, tomato and fennel bread, rye, parmesan, *focaccia,* hard-crusted, soft-bottomed, pancooked – it was getting worse than New York".

Annie laughed: "If you mentoned *focaccia* down here people would think you were being rude."

Peter enthused about the potatoes. "Back in Dublin, we used to buy these things loose, covered with soil, all kinds of sizes. I mean I suppose they were bursting with goodness and all that but they were so messy. Here in Ballybyug you buy your spuds in a handy plastic bag. I mean, what could be simpler?"

The Wayles were delighted too with the local workmen. Peter recalled how in his Dublin days even the heating installer had refused to do anything without an elaborate explanation of the environmental attractions of different systems. "I had to listen to a lot of hot air!" says Peter, who has even had his sophisticated sense of humour replaced with a simpler system on moving to the country. In Ballybyug "my man Joe just took one look at the house, plonked an almighty oil tank in the back garden, stuck a giant boiler in the shed, three radiators in every room and switched it all on – and it works. Annie was innocent enough to ask at the time about the effect on the environment, and do you know what Joe said? 'Sure haven't we a Minister to look after that?' I can tell you we found this sort of attitude very refreshing."

As for getting about in Ballybyug, the Wayles had discovered the simple pleasure of travelling by car. It was a revelation to them. For years they had accepted the quaint city notion that the only proper way to travel was on foot or by bicycle, but in Ballybyug they saw into their own hearts and bought a five-year old diesel car. "We're never as tired now as we used to be. It's a healthier way of life, letting a motor supply the energy."

Of course the real joy was in the people of the area, a community of perfectly normal human beings. "In Dublin we were surrounded by busybody neighbours who were always forming street communities, organising getting-to-know-you parties and so on. It drove us crazy. Here, the people keep to themselves. It's so *anonymous* – we love it."

With the huge success of *A Year in the Provinces,* however, the danger is that the area may become spoiled. Indeed the Belmullet peninsula, long noted for its authentic Spanish haciendas and American ranch spreads, is already dotted with newly whitewashed stone cottages as city dwellers move in, endangering the old way of life. But the Wayles are philosophic about the changes. At the time of writing they were packing for a two-week holiday in the Canaries: "That's another wonderful aspect of life here", mused Annie happily – "We don't feel we have to go on discovering the real Ireland any more now that we're part of it."

MANAGER OF THE WRITS HOTEL IN FRACAS

In March 1993, a well-known judge was arrested in an incident outside the locked doors of Dublin's Shelbourne Hotel, where he was seeking an after-hours drink.

The manager of the well-known Dublin hotel, The Writs, last night refused to apologise for an incident in which he was arrested outside the home of a High Court judge in the early hours of last Saturday while seeking after-hours legal advice.

The hotel manager, Stephen Green, last night issued a statement frankly admitting that he had "already had some legal advice" when he was arrested after Gardai were called to the judge's home at 1.45 am on Saturday. Mr Green said he was seeking "after-hours advice" following what he described as a "particularly stressful week's work". As was widely reported in the media, the manager had presided last week over some especially boisterous sessions in the hotel's popular Horse's Ass Bar, a favourite haunt of the legal profession, and had subsequently barred the participants for a period of seven days; a decision whose lenience was later heavily critised. Mr Green angrily contradicted an evening paper report which said no damage had been done to the door of the High Court judge's residence. "The facts are rather more sensational. After a particularly stressful week's work, I sought legal advice in the judge's residence after hours. I had already had some legal advice, in fact I had been on an all-day court crawl. The judge declined to answer the door, so I kicked it in. The Gardai were summoned and took me home. My wife then successfully pleaded with them to take me to the Bridewell. I have no regrets whatsoever because frankly, there's no such thing as bad publicity."

Certainly this scandalous episode will again draw attention to The Writs Hotel, where there have been numerous unsavoury incidents over the period since Mr Green's appointment as manager.

Stephen Green (38), whose name is regularly linked with top models Marion Rowe and Eli Place, is of course no stranger to controversy. A brilliant student at the Shannon Hotel Management School, his career initially took him all over the Munster hotel circuit, where he was involved in many critical and far-reaching decisions on the proper managing of hotels.

After a spell in Switzerland, Mr Green returned to a series of top management positions in Ireland's hotel industry, before being appointed to what is widely considered the most prestigious establishment in the country: certainly, there are few Dublin traditions which can compare with that of afternoon tea at The Writs.

Stephen Green first came to public notice in August 1992, when he was involved in a particularly contentious row over the correct alignment of dinner table napkins. Despite a spirited defence by traditionalists in the industry, Mr Green caught the national imagination with a famous victory: since then no five-star hotel has ever been seen to arrange its napkins with anything other than the "Green fold", as it came to be known.

However, it was Stephen Green's notably lenient treatment of unruly hotel guests and bar customers which first caused unease in the profession and in the public domain. While other managers were regularly barring offenders for long periods, Mr. Green rarely imposed anything more than the minimum exclusion period of one week. Yet the drink trade's self-policing body – the Bar Council – repeatedly refused to censure him.

We in the media, needless to say, are shocked and horrified that this kind of scandal should sully our pages and airwaves, and that the hotel industry should be dragged into disrepute by the indefensible actions of a small number of its members. Clearly however, such an incident should not be blown up out of proportion, a danger we advert to in editorial comment, opinion pieces by 19 of our columnists, details of a chess strategy once used by a third cousin of Mr. Green in an amateur competition in 1974, an analysis of how meteorological conditions can play havoc with decisions by people under pressure, the astrological conjunctions possibly affecting Mr Green's behaviour, a list of his hobbies, the names and addresses of his hotel management school colleagues, and where they are now; plus, in the sports supplement, an extended review of Mr Green's netball career.

It is our fervent hope that we shall hear no more of this unfortunate episode.

Scandal rocks the irish temporary

Early in 1993, the executive chairman of the Irish Permanent Building Society was suspended pending an investigation into financial transactions involving his Foxrock home.

Readers will be appalled to hear that I have been suspended from my position as executive chairman of the Irish Temporary Structure Society pending an investigation into transactions involving my Carrickmines cottage, *Sans Souci*; and subsidiary investigations involving my *pied-à-terre* in Percy Place, my villa in Castlegregory, my time-share in the Algarve, my ski-lodge in Klösters, my townhouse in Manhattan, my country seat in Cheshire, my shooting lodge in Nebraska, my winter residence in the Seychelles and my summer retreat in The Hamptons, Long Island.

I have of course every wish to set these matters straight, and accordingly I am bringing the matter to public attention solely in order to cover my ass, I beg your pardon, my assets, and to assure shareholders that the entire business while *sub judice* is above board.

The ITSS was set up at the turn of the century in response to the growing trend for erecting temporary structures of all kinds around the country, from school extensions to building-site canteens. Since then it has, I am proud to say, become the biggest temporary structure society in the country, with half a million customers and branches at almost every street corner.

I myself, may I say with all modesty, have contributed in no small way to the growth of the society since taking over the ITSS at the age of nine, when elected to the chairmanship on merit by the Cayman Islands holding group, Nepotism Unlimited, established by my father and grandfather.

There is no secret surrounding my arrangements with regard to *Sans Souci*. It is true, of course, that I made some elementary improvements to the cottage in question. Who among us can deny being just that little bit house-proud? I am no different from any other householder in this respect.

The facts are as follows. I bought *Sans Souci,* a modest 54-roomed cottage on 40 acres, on a lovely May morning in the 60s (how well I remember it!) for £24.89. That afternoon I negotiated a Home Improvement Loan from the Irish Temporary for £7 million, most of which went on the high-rise aquatic exercise facility (which the media in their usual snide manner prefer to call my "rooftop swimming pool"); the electrified fencing (Carrickmines suffers a serious ant infestation problem) and a battery of high-powered search-lights (my children are *forever* losing tennis balls).

The situation is really very simple, and it is only the financial media who are exaggerating this affair and suggesting Byzantine depths of money-dealing behind a straightforward acquisition-type arrangement, or what some people apparently refer to as a "purchase".

I bought the original property by means of a simple cash/asset barter exchange forward option delayed lease fixed interest ceiling inverse depreciation suspended clawback arrangement. This was not, as one newspaper has viciously suggested, a "no-lose" situation. In essence, it involved a simple trade-off wherein my services, or rather those of my one-man company Times Square Tax Wheeze, were made available to the ITTS in a strict time-ratio manner available for inspection in an open-book scenario to any shareholder with a flair for investigation and about three months to spare.

There were, naturally enough for a man in my position, some special arrangements. The unencumbered title of the property was vested, purely for security reasons, in the T-Square Tax Wheeze subsidary Maze Investments, of which I am (for my sins, as they say) executive chairman, managing director and sole shareholder. This company in turn subdivided the property rights among is its Golden group of spin-off companies, Golden Hellos, Golden Handcuffs, and – not quite finalised – Golden Parachutes, in all of which I am, as it happens, executive chairman, managing director and sole shareholder.

Because the matter is *sub judice* I can say no more. For any further comment, you are welcome to contact my legal adviser, Golden Words, of which, you may as well know, I am executive chairman, managing director and sole shareholder.

I will however say that there is too much begrudgery in this country for its own good, or, which is more to the point, for my own good.

CLERICAL ERRORS MAR KERRY TRAVELOGUE

In her book Forbidden Fruit, Annie Murphy told the scandalous story of her affair with Bishop Eamonn Casey.

The unprecedented demand for *Forbidden Fruit,* a first book by Irish-American author Annie Murphy, demonstrates once again the popular appeal of a good travelogue. And while the delights of a Kerry summer have attracted the interest of writers before, few authors have invested their books with such transparent passion as Ms Murphy. It can be only a matter of time before her remarkable account is on sale in every Bórd Fáilte office.

An unashamedly romantic memoir of a trip to Ireland undertaken by Ms Murphy in the sixties, the book wholeheartedly reflects the joyful liberation of the period. Certainly, following its publication, we are unlikely ever again to hear the cruel slur that Kerry was behind the times in embracing the so-called "permissive society" ushered in during those years. Indeed the book is, in a manner of speaking, packed with such embraces.

While some commentators are advancing *Forbidden Fruit* as another strong argument in favour of retaining the Shannon stopover, and others are drawing favourable comparisons with Edna O'Brien's *A Pagan Place,* Ms Murphy's book could perhaps more accurately be seen as a companion-piece to Corkery's *The Hidden Ireland.* Not for Annie Murphy, however, any leprechaunish musings about travelling by ass-cart around country boreens, dining on Irish stew or the like, although in the best traditions of rural Irish literature there are some vivid descriptions of ghostly late-night bedroom apparitions. No: Ms Murphy refuses to patronise us, instead taking an open pleasure in the sybaritic lifestyle offered to her in a county revealed as being full of surprises, almost as many of them for the native reader as for the visitor.

Ms Murphy recalls in detail her visits to a number of luxurious Irish establishments, where she regularly sampled the delights of fine wines and rich food, pure linen sheets and silk bedclothes. It is a pity however that the author, while describing the generous hospitality she enjoyed in these hitherto unpublicised retreats throughout the kingdom of Kerry and beyond, did not think to append an index of the establishments, their visitor accommodation and dining-room facilities. There must be numerous readers who would welcome the opportunity of trying them out.

Although Ms Murphy herself is the dominant personality of the book, mention must be made of her travelling companion, without whom many of her most enthralling experiences would quite possibly never have occurred. Acting as host and driver, historian and raconteur, personal assistant and guide to local wildlife, this quintessential Irishman unselfishly satisfied Ms Murphy's every desire. All young female American tourists should be so lucky. Perhaps at some stage he may bring himself to publish a companion-piece to Ms Murphy's volume? Reader interest could almost be guaranteed.

Unlike some more professional yet less caring travel writers, Annie Murphy kept in touch with those she had come to know and love in this country. She reveals through her writing a remarkable talent for forming close personal relationships, and maintaining them "across the miles". Certainly there must have been many a time in the intervening years when an Irish heart jumped as the phone rang and the joyful message was relayed – "It's Miss Murphy calling from Connecticut!"; and glorious Kerry days and nights were again recalled. In criticism, it must be pointed out that the book is marred by a number of clerical errors, and one is also compelled to wade through a great deal of extraneous material before being allowed to savour the many charming sidelights on a busy Kerry community life.

MY LIFE IN MOVIES

Neil Jordan's film The Crying Game won him an Oscar for best original screenplay.

A few years back, I was walking on Killiney Heath when I met a small friendly being from outer space, stranded on earth. No one believed me, of course, and a little later I misplaced my notes on the incident, which I had hoped to develop into a screenplay. Remarkably soon afterwards, I found the entire world was making its way to a production called *E.T* And yet at no time in the intervening period had Steven Spielberg made any attempt to contact me.

It is nice to see Neil Jordan winning an Oscar for a genuinely original screenplay, a rare commodity these days. As an old Hollywood hand I am, of course, long familiar with the scandal of plagiarism, and on a number of occasions have had to take issue with people who seemed intent on appropriating not only my stories, but even the incidents of my life.

As a rather serious young scriptwriter back in Los Angeles in the Twenties I recall, for example, jotting down a short, tightly-worded series of what one might call (though not to the face of a Hollywood agent) moral precepts, and what do you think happened? Yes: before I had gotten round to a first draft, Cecil B, as we all knew him then, was launching a rather bloated production called *The Ten Commandments.* Around the same time I was holidaying in Alabama and scribbled down a few notes about a sassy Southern belle who survived the Civil War but lost the only man she loved. *Taken on the Breeze* was my working title, but of course when David O got wind of it, his ego ordained there would be cosmetic changes. I have always felt his resulting saga was somewhat overwrought, though Clark and Vivien put in competent performances.

During the Twenties and Thirties I was more involved with the social side of Hollywood, making valuable contacts and so on. There were a lot of lunches, I recall. Then, one evening shortly after the war, I went out for a few drinks with my old pal Billy Wilder, who was beginning to make a bit of a name for himself in the directing racket. But I am sad to say that he took advantage of our little outing. The period we spent on the tiles was no more than about 36 hours, but then I suppose that as a title, *The Lost Weekend* was preferable to *The Lost Day and a Half.* There were liberties taken in the portrayal, too. You noted how Ray Milland, who even borrowed my famous slouch, drank on his own? That's not how I remember it, Billy!

In the same decade, while filling in a couple of months sprinkling stardust on other people's scripts, I became involved in a brief dalliance with an older lady, a well known actress of the silent screen. To my horror, a couple of years later, our brief encounter (itself a title casually appropriated by David Lean) was cruelly exposed in *Sunset Boulevard,* the title being Billy's droll way of drawing attention to the unfortunate lady's address on Moonrise Avenue. Of course in those days Hedda and Louella had their spies *everywhere.*

In search of a more cultural milieu in the early Fifties I found work as a newspaperman in Rome, where I hit it off with a young lady who turned out to have genuine blue blood. Being still relatively young and perhaps over-impressed with my aristocratic doxy, I told the story around. Next thing I knew the thing was up there on the big screen called, a bit on the literal side if you ask me, *Roman Holiday.* Gregory and Audrey were very good, of course, but there was more zing, if you get my drift, to the actual background.

Towards the end of the fifties I took a break from Hollywood and spent a short period leasing a rather lonely motel in the American south-west. It is true I was going through an bad emotional patch at the time, and also had to keep an eye on my mother, who was in the late stages of senile dementia. Even now, however, I cannot bring myself to mention, much less put on paper, the name of the crudely commercial film Mr Hitchcock spun from this episode. Anyone who wants to check the records will see that when not visiting Mother or my psychiatrist I ran a *totally* professional motel. There was another difficult period in my life when, under the pressures of my work in PR at the time, I sought solace in alcohol. Attempting a cure by means of the "share 'n' care" therapy fashionable at the time, my Norwegian wife June joined me in my aberration. Imagine then my horror a few months later when I went along to see something called *Days of Wine and Roses* (glad as I was to see my old friend "Manto" getting his song title on screen), expecting to see perhaps a nostalgic romance, and there was Lee Remick with *precisely* the same hairstyle as my (since estranged) wife June. And to think I valued the friendship of Blake Edwards.

You know, I have often told the tale (rather too often, I realise now) of how, when I was about 10 years old, my parents went off on holiday one Christmas with our extended family, and as a result of hectic last-minute preparations accidentally left me behind. Nothing more exciting happened while I was home alone but that some of the usual low-life called selling home-made wire artwork and the like. Still, you know the way stories get around and, in Hollywood, get hyped up. It's not that I plan to sue: I just wonder how Macaulay Culkin knew I had blond hair at his age.

HYNES TO DIRECT DRAMA AT FAIRYHOUSE

The 1993 Aintree Grand National was one of the biggest disasters in the history of racing, with the race cancelled after a false start warning went unnoticed by most of the field.

The Irish Grand National is over; it has already been run. The race to be seen at Fairyhouse this afternoon will be no more than an astoundingly clever and perfectly choreographed re-enactment, directed by Garry Hynes and featuring selected Abbey Players as jockeys. Trainers, breeders, owners and others in the know will play themselves, and all bets will be fully honoured, so that the punters will win or lose exactly what they would if the race were real. The actor-jockeys have signed legally-binding agreements to curb their natural enthusiasm during the event and eventually fall into the precise past-the-post order occurring during the real race, which took place over a specially-constructed steeplechase course on the beach in Inch, Co Kerry, at midnight on Saturday.

This incredible story is a direct result of the recent cock-up at Aintree. Immediately after the greatest disaster in the history of racing, a huge Irish organisation swung into action. There was, as one of the trainers explained, no way in which Ireland could risk a similar disaster – never mind risk vindicating a British trainer's assertion that we are "a backward little country". Clearly, too much was at stake. Accordingly, under conditions of the strictest secrecy, the Irish Grand National was run under cover of darkness, with Inch strand an obvious venue because of its well-established reputation for strange nocturnal comings and goings, of which nobody takes much notice any more. The race itself went perfectly. There were no problems at the start, there was no need for any heart-stopping recalls. There was joy, there was ecstasy. There were disappointed people too, of course, but that is the nature of racing.

It was, I can tell you now, a nailbiting affair. Naturally I am sworn to silence on the results, but it was a very close-run thing. I can confess to actually envying those viewing today's performance for the first time.

For this afternoon's event at Fairyhouse will undoubtedly prove the greatest outdoor drama ever staged in Irish history. If all goes according to plan, it will copperfasten the reputation of Garry Hynes, who strenuously denies that today's race has anything to do with her planned departure from the Abbey. Nevertheless, rumours that Ms Hynes has succumbed to the lure of racing have swept the artistic and equestrian worlds, and – capitalising on the fact that she weighs scarcely six stone – that she is to begin training as a National Hunt jockey.

Having been a privileged spectator behind the scenes for some time now, I can confidently challenge anyone to identify any of the well-known Abbey actors in their lookalike jockey roles today. Certainly, in the dress rehearsal at Inch they were all totally convincing in their silks and boots and cute little caps, a walking (and sometimes trotting) tribute to the Abbey's wardrobe mistress and the make-up team, all of whom faced, and overcame, the severest test in their careers.

The entire daring concept was kept under wraps until the actors arrived at Inch. When the truth was revealed, the excitement among them was palpable, and while the riding instructors employed for the occasion were kept busy, it was no time at all before the entire troupe was affecting a quite professional bowlegged appearance.

After the race proper, which the players greatly enjoyed (indeed John Kavanagh opened a small but successful book on the outcome) the video was replayed to the assembled troupe of thespians, and casting quickly began. There was naturally great competition for the plum role of winning jockey, and those who auditioned were tried out in the winner's enclosure to test their victory speech for proper balance, i.e. the mixture of pride, joy, modesty, acknowledgement of the horse's contribution, due deference to the trainer and/or owner, and downright servility.

Obviously, those in the know at Fairyhouse today include all the jockeys, trainers and organisers, and the actors and actresses. Look out too for a well-disguised Michael Colgan in a very important role. I am unable to reveal what it is, but as a hint I can remind you that he has got more successful productions off to a perfect start than anyone else in the game. Enough said. Noel Pearson has already secured the rights to this incredible story. *Dancing at Lughnasa* will, he says excitedly, be nothing compared to *Fooling at Fairyhouse,* his provisional title for the stage production on which Eoghan Harris is already working, and the follow-up film to be directed by Neil Jordan. We may be backward, we Irish, but by God we're not stupid.

WRITE AND GET PAID (MORE) FOR IT

In April 1993 the author Gordon Thomas tracked down Bishop Eamonn Casey to his South American hideaway and then produced a long newspaper "interview" subsequently disowned and denied by the Bishop.

Garvan Thomson, the reclusive author whose recent breakthrough in the Bishop affair had the Irish journalistic world reeling with envy and admiration, has been tracked down to a remote monastery in Wicklow, where he is undergoing an intensive course in English before departing for the Money-Making Missions. The monastery monks have apparently run off to find a secret hideaway of their own. From the moment I departed the *Irish Times* offices, clutching my commission for a five-figure sum (£5) I was determined to catch up with the man.

I began by unravelling the web of travel arrangements through old Dublin Bus schedules, bribing a series of rural hackney drivers and taping a phone-call between Thomson and an intinerant out of-work woodcutter who once shared an apartment with the author, and was now ready to do anything for a few bob.

It took a long time – nearly two hours, in fact, but perseverance is the mark of the true journalist. For the last leg of my trip I chartered a small plane and arrived on the outskirts of the village of Enniskerry. From there I hacked my way through about half a mile of undergrowth and suddenly found myself in a small clearing. And there stood Garvan Thomson. "I'm gobsmacked" he said, as much in admiration as in surprise. Having been thus provided with the substance of a 10,000-word interview, I can tell you I was one happy journalist.

As with the bishop, recent events have had their effect on Thomson. Gone is the unhealthy pallor of a writer out of the publicity spotlight and off the front pages of newspapers for too long. Gone is the hungry look of a man who hasn't had a major scoop for years. Gone too is the nervous tic of a man unable to convince a newspaper that his expenses are justified. Time now to finish that paragraph and start a new one. Garvan Thomson has removed his beard and put on 30 pounds. In appearance he is now heavier and less hairy.

While it may not seem necessary to have actually written this last sentence, provided you read the one preceding it, the point is that in your eagerness to hear more of the man, you have hardly noticed the repetition, whereas I, on the other hand, have filled another few lines with perhaps 50 or 60 words and am thus getting that little bit closer to a long, perhaps even a really long article, which is obviously and clearly and transparently important when one has an agreement, gilt-edged of course, to be paid by the word. Or the words, which is three more. (Ten now, actually).

I learned these useful tricks of the journalistic trade by attending the lectures Thomson delivers in his spare time. And to give the man his due, I can heartily recommend his accompanying book, *How to Succeed in Journalism without Really Prying*.

Thomson was so impressed that I had discovered his hideaway – just the sort of practical exercise he often sets his students – that as a reward, he generously allowed me to sit in on some of his lectures.

These covered all the essential areas of journalism: Deal-making, Phone-tapping, Deal-making, Mind-reading, Denial (including Counter-denial), Deal-making, Hyperbole (and its Superb, Wonderful, Amazing Advantages), Tautology (Let Me Repeat That), Invention (as the Mother of Necessity), Invention (Pure), Lying (Low), Deal-making, Fact-finding (optional), Story Development and Journalistic Standards, wittily sub-titled "You want ethics, you go to Maynooth".

Subsidiary courses for would-be press photographers include Deal-Making, Car Handbrake Turns, Deal-making, Outdoor Pursuits and Deal-Making.

When I asked about lectures on actually writing, Mr Thomson said anyone could write, so there was little point in wasting valuable lecture-time. One could see what he meant.

Anyway, I put all the Thomson precepts into action straightaway, and you are reading the result. I admit I am rather proud of it, considering as it is being the first article what I have wrote.

Rising to the cognac challenge

Browsing recently through the reading material in my dentist's waiting-room (wasn't it awful about the *Titanic?*) I came across a marvellous magazine advertisement for a certain brand of cognac. "Have you thrown a party that friends still talk about?" it archly queried. "Ever crewed a yacht beyond the sight of land? Have you ever received a standing ovation?"

The intimation was that even if one couldn't answer "yes" to all of these questions, the choice of this particular brand of booze ("A taste for life") would straightaway align one with those who can: the wonderful, successful, celebrated, go-ahead, talented, individualist, witty, influential, clever, creative, sophisticated, charming, desirable, rich, attractive, healthy, pencil-slim cellulite-free villa-owning au-pair-possessing chaffeur-driven power-encrusted blow-dried mahogany-tanned flat-stomached muscle-tautened skin-toned collagen-enhanced hormone-treated face-lifted nose-straightened breast-augmented lipo-suctioned colon-irrigated hair-transplanted eyelash-tinted nail-extended penile-implanted designer-dressed brilliant blonde unblemished breath-taking glittering glamorous glowing glorious, deliriously happy and utterly enviable Beautiful People.

Drink this particular brandy, the subliminal message promises, and you can be one of them.

Let others mock if they will. Left on the outside long enough, I decided to give the stuff a lash. What was there to be lost? Perhaps nothing more than a few illusions. And to be gained? With luck, an entrée to this most exclusive club. It seemed a fair gamble. So off I went to my local boozer.

They had to send out for the stuff. When it arrived a small crowd of regulars, pint-drinkers to a man, gathered around as the barman, with professionally restrained derision, poured out a measure. Everybody stared at the beautiful golden liquid as it lay there, haughty and serene, in the glass. But not very high up in the glass. "Better make it a double, Joe" I said purposefully. The second measure stirred up a brief ferment, then all that was left on the smooth gilded surface was one tiny bubble.

I drank it, and ate the bubble. It was beautiful: like dying and going to Heaven. I cannot say I immediately felt glamorous, but the glow was unmistakable.

"What you want with that stuff is a chaser," said someone who apparently knew about these things. So I had a pint. It felt strange, the sensation of the heavy black porter cascading over the golden grape juice distillation, but somehow, *right.*

Wrong. Some hours later, after a few more of these double-brandy and pint chaser combinations, I spontaneously issued a general invitation to an impromptu party in the well-known Sandycove lodgings. Unfortunately, it turned out to be even more impromptu than planned, so to speak, and all the drink in the house disappeared within half an hour. My companions departed in that lofty Mylesian vehicle, high dudgeon, and swore they would not forget. Then it was that I recalled the first question on the cognac advertisement: had I thrown a party that friends still talk about? Undoubtedly.

But now I was firmly in the grip of a strange euphoria, and despite the darkness of the night I felt the irresistible lure of the ocean. Only close contact with the sea could, I realised, satisfy this powerful craving. So I climbed into my small boat, handily moored at the end of my seaside garden, and began to row.

I rowed for hours, until my strength gave out. As I sank exhausted into the stern, it suddenly occurred to me I might well have fulfilled the second challenge of the brandy advertisement and crewed my yacht, well, rowed my row-boat, out of sight of land. At any rate, land was definitely out of sight of me, and that was practically the same thing.

When I awoke, it was morning. I rose unsteadily from the stern of the boat and looked around. Now I discovered why the rowing had been so exhausting. I had forgotten to undo the moorings, and was exactly three metres – the length of the mooring line – from where I had set out. Shielding my eyes from the morning sun, I noticed a small crowd of people gathered at the end of the garden. My friends, concerned at my state of mind on the previous night, had returned, and now, to a man, they rose and applauded. Yes, the third brandy challenge had been successfully taken up: I was receiving a standing ovation

I stepped overboard, squelched my way shakily to dry land and was heartily congratulated by my companions. You would hardly have thought it to look at me, but I had been subsumed into the ranks of the Beautiful People.

PARENTING: THE CRAIC IS UP TO 90

In the whole fascinating area of modern-day parenting, the contribution that young people can make has been unaccountably overlooked. Herewith, then, for those too young to remember when "parent" was a noun, some guidelines which may prove useful.

Coping with Rejection. Your parents will often be moody and difficult. They are experiencing feelings of being hopelessly, confused, bewildered and rejected. In most cases, the reason is simple enough: your parents *are* hopelessly confused, bewildered and rejected. This will regularly be the case even when they have *not* been drinking. (see below) A parent's mind is, at the best of times, a delicate mechanism, and frankly there isn't much you can do, short of giving your parents a good shake once in a while. However, an occasional affectation of concern will not go astray either. But don't over-do it.

Sexual Development. This is a tricky area. The longer your parents have been married, the more difficult it will be to convince them that males and females are not entirely different species. Your attempts to bring up "the physical side of things" (it is as well to use phrases they understand) will often meet with blank stares and/or foolish nostalgic grins. Take things gently. Their bodies are undergoing rapid change, with total collapse imminent. If you can't be sympathetic, fake it.

Peer Pressure. Some parents do better than others, and unfortunately the others always seem to include yours. Still, you will want to impress your parents with the need to develop to their full potential, even if it is painfully obvious they haven't got any. So keep up the pressure on the pair with which you are lumbered, and who knows, no matter how hopeless they appear to you, they may yet get job promotion, learn how to tell jokes properly, and give up their pathetic attempts to look good in denim.

Pocket Money. Sit down with your parents, agree a fixed amount weekly and under no circumstances give them any more. (In all areas of parenting, it is important to establish parameters). Profligacy is commonplace among parents, most of whom will have long histories of spending more than they earn. It is important for your own welfare as well as theirs that you do not encourage this habit, at least when the unearned money is not being spent on you.

Drinking. Parents learn by example, so what is important here is your own attitude. Accordingly, if you see them drunk, try to disguise your natural apathy. Remember that a concerned attitude will induce guilt on their part, and a guilty parent is a good parent. Well, most of the time.

Schooling. Your parents will be full of talk each autumn about the various adult education courses available. Do not undermine their fragile egos by reminding them of their notorious educational failures when they were your age, or of how they dropped out of the previous year's course after one class. Encourage them. Parents are by nature frail, insecure creatures, and you must beware of undermining their self-confidence. Anyway, it will get them out from under your feet.

Holidays. You will regularly hear your parents moaning about how their friends go on regular trips abroad, and how *they* never get to go anywhere. Ignore all such complaints. Refuse to be influenced by the alleged arrangements in other households. Similarly ignore the annual plans for boring family holidays. Suggest to your parents that they go away for a week or two without you: they will make a big fuss, but insist that you can get along for a little while on your own. They are of course, in their pathetically obvious way, only trying to protect your feelings, so you just do the same for them, and all will be well.

Behavioural Problems. You will often see your parents curse the world (in hopelessly dated slang), throw tantrums, fight with each other, kick the cat and generally misbehave. These are no more than attention-seeking ploys, and honestly, the best response is none at all. Simply take no notice. Just remember that your parents are just going through difficult years, and that as parents, these are the only kind of years they will have.

Parents can be a joy, but getting the best out of a mother and father has never been easy. Nevertheless, with good parenting they should give years of pleasure and useful service. As they age, the fruit of your labours will gradually become evident, and you will be able to take pride in their development. Good luck.

U2 CAN SHARE THE EXPERIENCE

"Instead of moving the full 50-strong Macnas company around Europe, U2 and the troupe came up with the clever idea of using only 12 members of the company, and relying on the local U2 fan clubs of all the cities visited to produce 100 extra members of the cast on a volunteer basis. This provides a nice way of offering added value to U2 fans ('Hey kids! Why just see the Zooropa tour when you can actually be the Zooropa tour!') while actually saving money."

– (Report in *The Irish Times*)

Clever idea? Listen: this is nothing short of a cultural breakthrough. So it is surely only fitting that it should come from the cultural icon of U2 itself, and that the group and its management should, in these straitened times, show such concern for saving money (well, their own) by clever use of resources (well, other people's) and all in the selfless cause of offering "added value" (well, unpaid work) to enthusiastic young people (possibly including yours).

Anyway, I decided to apply this remarkable new principle of work creation/cash conservation to one of my own projects, Central Abbatoirs, where construction is about to begin. Outside the site stood the usual pathetic group of jobless, in the forlorn hope of a start, and I began without preamble. "Hey kids!" I cried, though in truth, their average age was about 52, "Why just *see* this state-of-the art abbatoir network come into being when you can actually be *part* of it, share in its creation?"

I am sorry to say my enthusiasm was greeted with suspicious looks, and a good deal of angry muttering. After some time, one man stepped forward and asked, very bluntly I must say, if I was offering them jobs.

Well, it may be that I haven't got Bono's charisma, or Paul McGuinness's acumen. But I did my best to explain that while I could not offer them *jobs,* which would be in crude contravention of this new principle of employment, I was offering them *work.* I became enthusiastic – perhaps over-so, emphasising the delights of being *part of the experience.* Just as old-timers recall Woodstock, or the Isle of Wight, or Monterey, and proudly claim they were present, so too could these men, in years to come, point out Central Abbatoirs to their grandchildren and quietly boast: "I was part of it; I was there."

My logic, and my oratory, were lost on them. No longer possessing the uncluttered minds of their youth, they could not grasp the concept. And of course when people fail to understand a new concept, they often become angry. Some of them, believe it or not, just walked away from this rare chance of participating in a genuinely groundbreaking cultural-fiscal event.

I had a sudden inspiration. I asked the dwindling crowd if they would be more prepared to participate if I presented them with, at practically cost price, a T-shirt each, in pure cotton-type fabric, with *Central Abbatoirs* emblazoned back and front! Again they were unreceptive. Indeed one of them said, and you will find this hard to credit,"So as well as working for nothing, you want us to provide free advertising too?"

There isn't much you can do with people so out of touch as this.

The layabouts began to drift away, still muttering angrily, and I had almost given up hope when one of the younger men stepped forward and asked me for a few moments in private. I assented; and I can tell you now how glad I am I did so, for Joe turned out to be a man of rare vision.

My abbatoir project is coming along nicely these days, though it's a little unfortunate that the youngsters working free for us – I beg your pardon, sharing the experience, can't start until they finish school each day. They tend to lose their strength fairly quickly too, I notice. But they *adore* being part of a cultural mega-event in the humane animal slaughter field, and it's a joy to see them beavering away in their project T-shirts. It was Joe who convinced me that as a logo, *Rivers of Blood 1993* had a better zing to it than *Central Abbatoirs*. Joe is, I can tell you, a truly brilliant merchandising manager, and he runs the various concessions from T-shirts to posters to the canteen, as well as being in charge of *I'll Scratch Yours,* our much-admired international press massaging operation.

At this stage, the pop music industry could probably learn a thing or two from us. Indeed, Joe is already sketching out a reasonably-costed instruction programme. Speaking of sketches, I would advise anyone thinking of bidding for our unique abbatoir art concession to move fast.

THE ASCENT OF NEW MAN MOUNTAIN

In 1993, The Irish Times reported from Mount Everest on the first successful attempt on the mountain by an Irish team.

More difficult than Everest, more dangerous than K2, more sublime than the Matterhorn. You will have heard much of mountaineering feats in recent weeks, but perhaps little or nothing of the handful of sensitive male souls who have actually reached the summit, and perched modestly on the pinnacle, of New Man Mountain.

There were just six of us involved in this hazardous expedition, sponsored by Safe Harbour Bonding, the Inner Feelings Foundation and Ovaltine. Location back-up came from a team of 30 powerfully-built female Sherpas, without whom our equipment, never mind our consciousness, could ever have been raised.

Before we left there was, as you can imagine, much hugging and kissing. Then the six of us, Reginald, Timothy, Jonathan, Tarquin, Joe and myself, separated briefly to say goodbye to our loved ones. The tears flowed freely; a good augur, we agreed.

Arriving at Camp Cry-baby, as one of the needlessly cynical female Sherpas christened it, we could hardly wait to get started on our first interpersonal connection session. Timothy began, in his attractive whisper, by telling us of his early years, when his mother brought him up, healthy and happy, certainly – but never gave him special time. We all burst into tears immediately, and had to have a consoling cup of Ovaltine, and a nice piece of Tarquin's delicious home-made quiche lorraine. Timothy got hugged to *bits,* I can tell you.

Jonathan then confessed how he felt disconnected from his emotional capacity, and how his initiation into manhood had left him vulnerable, hurt, shivering, small. At just five feet, Jonathan actually *is* somewhat on the small side, but I need hardly tell you none of us would ever mention the fact.

It was late when we got to bed, but holding hands together outside our sleeping bags we sang the night away. I don't mind confessing that we were *jelly* after Tarquin's ever-so-gentle rendition of *Over the Rainbow.*

Next morning, after hugging some more, we pressed on. All around us in the snow lay distressing evidence of previous ill-fated expeditions, with deserted bonding harbours, abandoned masculinity realignment workshops and shattered sensitivity nourishment centres everywhere. We felt sad – but we were grateful for the feeling.

Higher and higher we climbed, breathing in the rarefied air of emotional/psychosexual replenishment, until finally, exhausted, we reached Camp Consolation. It was time for more Ovaltine, and Tarquin toasted lots of "soldiers" to dip in our boiled eggs. We then sat around our little fire while Reginald held us spellbound, for five hours, with an extremely personal exploration of how he came to reject his imposed masculine identity. He felt alienated from his self, he explained in his rather high-pitched voice. He had difficulties with intimacy; he was denied his fullness, his oneness, his very mode of being. Poor Reggie: he loosened the warm woollen cravat his mummy had knitted him and the tears flowed freely.

We all lay down flat on the snow and touched fingers, in a circle, with poor damaged Reggie in the middle. You should have seen us, bonding there silently in the moonlight, with just a stray yak or two for company, and the awesome North Col of New Man Mountain looming above. It was not a sight one could easily forget.

Next morning, before our attempt (I reject the crudely aggressive word "assault") on the summit, we decided we should first commune with the mountain itself, to get in sympathy with its inner nature, its mountainness. But just as we knelt down, tragedy struck: about three tons of snow suddenly fell from an overhanging ledge right on top of Timothy. Joe said later, rather insensitively I thought, that the mountain had obviously decided to commune with *us*. Poor Timothy; but we all knew he would have enjoyed going like that, suffocating under a blanket of virgin snow. There was something so right about it.

We stumbled on.

Joe and I were eventually chosen for the first dash to the summit. I had begun to have my doubts about Joe, whose masculinity seemed suspiciously robust, and sadly, I was proved right. At the very last moment he ran ahead of me, gained the summit and absolutely screamed: "Made it Ma, top of the world!"

It was awful to see a man fail at the very last moment, but as leader there was no way I could tolerate such crass male pride in achievement. The fact that Joe had called on his mother was a mitigating factor, but not sufficiently so. I even tried mouth-to-mouth counselling, but it was no use – Joe didn't really really really want to change.

There comes a time when even a New Man has to do what a man has to do; and so, on the pretence of hugging him, I pushed Joe firmly over the precipice.

"Wimps!" I could hear him scream, as he took the fastest way down. "Wimps, all of you!"

On the descent, we suggested bonding with our female sherpas, but somehow they got the wrong idea. Clearly, even New Man Mountaineers as experienced as ourselves can still make the odd mistake.

THE PLAYGOER'S THE THING – UNFORTUNATELY

With Alan Ayckbourn's play *Just Between Ourselves* having just concluded its run at the Gate, it seems an appropriate time to take issue with one of the eminent playwright's remarks. "All this modern stuff" he has been quoted as saying "three people dressed entirely in black point at the audience accusingly for 10 minutes – only baffles the customers."

Speaking as the author of some 139 stage plays (137 of them admittedly unproduced) which open with precisely this scene, or a minor variation thereof, I am saddened, though not altogether surprised, at Alan's dismissive attitude. We modern playwrights are used to such slander, and bear it as stoically as we can. There comes a time, however, when a defence must be made.

The most depressing aspect of theatre today is of course the utter inadequacy and hopelessness of audiences, with their pathetic need to be "entertained", their naive demands for "good plots", a so-called "variety of characters" and of course the "odd laugh" as they ignorantly like to put it. In short, these people seem to regard the most demanding and agonised creation on the part of artists like myself merely as an excuse for a "good night out" on theirs.

Clearly a good deal of re-education is necessary, not to mention a major shift in cultural attitudes. After all, I myself can vouch for the fact that even the most brilliantly gifted playwright is obliged to put in many years of hard work before producing genuine artistic gems. So what sort of foolish confidence makes theatre-goers think they can just walk into a theatre, without any preparation, other than perhaps having just put their odious children to bed, and expect to acquit themselves with any distinction?

Alan Ayckbourn, poor fellow, has only himself to blame for his material success. Behind him, and presumably ahead of him too, lies an embarrassing string of runaway successes, of full houses. Those of us in DAFT (Defence of Alienation For the Theatre) warned him of the dangers of popular acclaim, but he refused to listen. At this stage, of course, he is probably past redemption.

We DAFT members, on the other hand, retain the great and priceless gift of illusion. For after all, what have we to believe in if *not* illusion, if you will permit me to coin a typical phrase of alienation? I have always felt that the child who pointed out that the Emperor had no clothes showed a sad lack of imagination. What kind of a home must such a little horror have come from, that he could destroy with such heartless cruelty the magnificent illusion of gold apparel? It sometimes seems to me that today's theatre audiences are made up entirely of this little brat's descendants.

I am well aware there were problems, in terms of production, with some of my plays. And indeed on occasion, with my script, my characters, my settings, my lighting requirements, my special effects, and most of my other stage needs. But what was I to do, compromise? When my play *Stop Or You Live* demanded a cast of precisely 2,345 characters, as it did, what should I have done? Shrug my shoulders, shake hands with the producer, and settle for the seven he offered? This same philistine had the gall to assert that apart from the "prohibitive" cost, no stage could possibly accommodate so many people. "Then build one" was my spirited response at the time, an answer which I believe will be applauded by anyone genuinely appreciative of true art.

It is true that my plays do tend to create confrontational situations *vis-a-vis* the audience, but this is merely my way of challenging their perceptions. And perhaps on occasion the difficulties were partially of my own creation. But it was hardly all my fault that during the only production of *One Last Gasp,* when, as my stage instructions demanded, 38 members of the audience were bound by whipcord to their seats, gagged and verbally abused, that one should have had a fatal heart attack. It did not in the least invalidate the play's thesis. Indeed it was wonderfully ironic, given the play's title, and merely underlined the whole thrust of my creation.

I can still feel a keen sense of disappointment at the man's family being under-impressed by these arguments of mine at the time. And when the other 37 theatre-goers subsequently sued for damages, I knew there still remained a great deal of educational work to be done.

FOR GOD'S SAKE, LET MY MONIES GO

The Tax Amnesty plan by the Government in 1993 drew a lot of criticism.

The human monetary rights organisation Tax Amnesty International (TAI) is mounting a campaign for the release of Irish hot money accounts from foreign banks infamous for their harsh security and unbending secrecy. Switzerland has been specifically targeted, since conditions in its bank cells – or "vaults", to use the preferred euphemism – are particularly notorious. All its grossly overfed bank accounts, many of them languishing there for years, are kept in complete isolation, and referred to by the Armani-suited "screws" only by number, never by name.

By posing as a speculative investor, and speaking only in terms of multi-million pound sums, I managed to secure a secret interview with one such hapless victim in a leading Zurich bank. The plight of account number 88153456972 has already been highlighted by TAI, which has selected him as its Prisoner of the Month.

When I came face to face with 88153456972, he was friendly, but guarded. "You can call me 88," he began. "That's what all you friends call you, is it?" I said, trying to put him at his ease. "No," he replied, "but if I had any friends, that's what I hope they would call me."

The physical conditions in which 88 is kept could hardly be faulted. Though security is tight, the entire area is spotlessly clean, while air-conditioning keeps all accounts at a controlled temperature, incidentally making a cod of the name "hot" money.

But straightaway one could see evidence of severe psychological damage. Poor 88 had been there five years, and the agony was clearly unbearable. The unhealthy pallor of unused £500 notes was an immediate giveaway, and despite the air-conditioning, 88 was sweating thousands as he talked.

"For the record," I began, my notebook at the ready, "what exactly is it you want?" 88 shuddered: "Please don't use the word record," he said pitifully, "and for God's sake don't take any notes."

It was immediately clear that the atmosphere had tainted his very soul.

After a pause, 88 went on: "My desires are simple. I want to get out of this Swiss hell-hole. I want to go back to Ireland. I want to contribute. I want to be *spent*. I am an innocent accumulation of surplus cash and I do not deserve to be let languish here indefinitely"

At this stage, 88 briefly broke down in tears. He then apologised, and blew his nose on a small-denomination note. We asked how he had been treated. Had he been fed properly? "Oh yes. I receive regular interest – I've actually got much fatter here." Eight-eight managed a weak smile. He was worried however about the forced diet that might ensue if he was ever repatriated. When we assured him that under proposed new rules, his body weight would be decreased by a mere 15 per cent, he was ecstatic. Would it be a once-off loss? Yes, that was the promise. Would the weight ever go on again in Ireland? We suppressed a laugh, assured him it was quite impossible, and changed the subject.

Then 88 told us of his youth. He had grown up in a small town in Ireland, living "a sort of Robin Hood existence". We pointed out that the latter robbed the rich to help the poor. "To help the *who?*" he inquired, with interest so substantial as to verge on the compound.

But he was an outsider, the subject of jealousy and spite, with the hurtful stigma of illegitimacy always attaching to him. "I moved in the dark, spurned by Ordinary Incomes, just because I was bigger and fatter. They were irreparably stunted, of course, because of regular beatings with savage instruments of torture. I don't even like to mention them."

"Taxes?" we ventured. "Yes", said 88, shuddering. "and when I saw everyday brutalities like this inflicted, I grew more and more fearful for my own life. So I hid away, getting fatter and fatter."

"Ah, cruel fate," I whispered consolingly. "Accrual fate, more accurately," corrected 88. "And finally, when I got too fat to be successfully hidden any longer, I was sent to Switzerland. So here I am, as you can see, a huge heap of untouchable cash. You know, I grew up in Catholic Ireland, but God forgive me, the truth is I just don't *want* to be saved – I want to be spent.

"I'm not asking much, if you think about it: just to be taken home, to walk in the sunlight, mix with Ordinary Incomes and not be shunned. I have a lot to offer. Well, 15 per cent. After all, the last thing I would want is to encourage greed."

AROUND THE WORLD IN 80 CLICHÉS

A mere seven weeks after leaving his Sallynoggin home for a round-the-world voyage estimated to take three months, solo yachtsman Noah Swallow eased his 30-foot ketch, *It's a Doddle,* into Dun Laoghaire harbour yesterday evening. Sporting a well-pressed navy suit, an immaculate white shirt and a red bow-tie, Swallow looked fit and well, and claimed to have put on 30 pounds during his trip.

Indeed, when the yachting press arrived, confidently expecting to see a broken shell of a man, and eager to hear his tales of shipwreck, suffering, loneliness and starvation, they instead found Swallow relaxing on deck with a glass of champagne and a bowl of chilled beluga caviar.

Sadly then, Swallow proved quite unable to live up to the reporters' expectations. To their astonishment and displeasure, he protested that his trip had been quite uneventful, indeed downright boring. And he apologised for his inability to provide them with tales of seafaring distress with which they might regale their readers.

It was Aloysius "Mainbrace" Moran, the thrusting new pen at *Boats and Bilge*, who decided straight away that Swallow was not going to be allowed off the hook so easily. "Look here Swallow,", said Moran forcefully, "you've just sailed around the world, and it simply isn't possible that you survived without at least losing your mast, or your sail, or both."

Swallow nodded animatedly: he had indeed, he admitted, lost both mast and sail. The press relaxed a little. Swallow then explained how he had read on innumerable occasions of solo sailors "limping" home to port with a makeshift mast and a tiny piece of material, "usually a torn shirt or blanket," functioning as a sail. The reporters nodded enthusiastically. "Well", explained Swallow, "I decided that I would actually *set out* with a makeshift mast – a used broomstick, actually, and an old shirt – and keep my *new* mast and sail for any emergency."

There was a shocked silence before the *Spinnaker* correspondent, Meredith "Sixpack" Staunton, stood up: "And exactly what purpose did this serve?" he enquired coldly. "Well", replied Swallow politely, "it simply meant than when my makeshift mast and sail were blown away, just beyond Cape Horn as it happened – I was able to replace them with my *new* equipment. Take a look – oh dear, silly of me – I've forgotten to remove the price tags."

The reporters watched, dumbstruck, as Swallow removed the Texas Homecare stickers from his immaculate mast and sail. John B "Sloop" Crosbie of *The Tiller* then rose purposefully to his feet. "Look, Swallow. No one sails around the world without capsizing. So even if nothing else happened, you *must* have capsized. Are you going to deny it?"

"Oh no," replied Swallow eagerly. "In fact I capsized six times."

"So at least you did something right," sneered Crosbie.

"Yes," mused Swallow, "you see I studied other round-the world sailors' accounts and I found the average number of capsizes was four. So just before I sailed out of Dun Laoghaire harbour, I deliberately capsized the boat five times – and once more for luck."

"And this worked?" gasped Crosbie.

"Oh yes. After all, have you ever heard of someone capsizing more than six times?"

"Well, no," said Crosbie weakly.

"There you are then."

"But your rations, your water supply!" shrieked Guy "Spinnaker" Connors of the monthly *All At Sea*, "you must have had problems there!"

"Oh", said Swallow, "you mean was I reduced to eating plank beetles and drinking my own urine? Well yes, actually. But once I realised there was really no way to avoid this, I decided to get it over with at the outset. So that was my diet for the first four days, but afterwards I really lived rather well." Swallow paused: "Would any of you care for a little caviar, or a drop of champagne ?"

Rupert "Heineken" Horan of *Ocean Wave* magazine made a last effort on behalf of his demoralised colleagues. "Swallow. Out there alone on the ocean, under the sky and the myriad stars and the vast elemental emptiness, surely there were times when you felt you were going mad ?"

Swallow grew pensive. "I *did* become worried about my state of mind at one point", he admitted, "but I recovered once I stopped reading the memoirs of round-the-world solo yachtsmen."

"You won't be writing an account of your trip, then ?" asked Horan mournfully.

"I'm afraid not," replied Swallow kindly. "What would be the point? It's all been rather dull, as you can see. I suppose you could say I was dogged by a catalogue of success."

VERSE IS YET TO COME

The singer-songwriter Sinead O'Connor was in the news, literally, when she took out a full page in The Irish Times to deliver her poetic thoughts on being a "child-adult."

I am not Sinéad O'Connor
Which is probably just as well
One Sinéad is quite enough
To be going on with. I am not an adult-child or a child-adult either:
I am a parent-adult
God help me.

It's a hard thing to be these days
And not getting any easier. Only other parent-adults know my pain
They too are child abuse victims
Yet our abuser-children walk free in the sun.

A parent-adult is a pitiable thing
Full of inner weakness.
All its strength has been sucked out by child-thingies.
It can never be replaced.

The baby-child is the pits. It drains your energy like a sponge
You lavish care on it and haul
Home gigantic packs of Pampers
Until you wish the baby not the nappy were disposable.
Then you feel guilty. Your baby-child
Has the upper hand and you
Are under it for ever.

Children cause all the problems of the world – like famine.
The teen-child devours a week's shopping in a day
Child-adults my granny; these are child-locusts
They empty fridges with fearful speed.
They hoover up food but never the floor.

There is no law against children
Because children make the laws.
Sinead speaks of the child within;
It is the child without that drives you bonkers.

Speaking out is dangerous.
Why do you think The Irish Times employs no children?
Because it knows fear. That's why.
Children buy it for their parents in the newsagent, but they will usally get
some sweets too.
That's how they operate.
Manipulation is their middle name.

Children take all your time
And never have any. You have to ferry them around.
Their favourite words are
Go, get, give, want and buy.
That is their vocabulary
And their life
Limited by your pathetic wallet
So as usual it's your fault
You restrict and ruin their lives
Because you are an adult-parent.
You creep.
And your offspring are child-monsters.

You will be a parent-adult forever.
Think about it.
The death penalty is reversible
But nothing is done about the sentence of parent-adulthood.
Which is irreversible.
It isn't fair.

The adult-child is worst of all.
He won't leave home, the lump.
The empty nest syndrome is for him nothing but an ornithological phenomenon
And you wait in vain.

The only hope of the parent-adult is revenge.
The hope that your child-thingies will one day grow up
Though you would not think it now.
But inside every child-thingy
Is a parent-adult-thingy waiting
To be born. If you tell them this
They will laugh yet you will have
The last laugh. But only if you last long enough.

COPING WITH THE CARAVANNING EXPERIENCE

You will often hear people going on about how much the whole nature of camping and caravanning has changed, and how the average campsite stay is now supposedly as luxurious as a sojourn in a five-star hotel. Going by recent caravanning experience, however, I have to say the comparison is a little exaggerated.

It is true, of course, that in comparison with times gone by, caravanners today are pampered beyond belief, with showers and flush toilets and on-site electricity and hair-dryers and barbeques and patio furniture and fridges and heaters. One is so much at home that one is given to wondering why one ever *left* home.

And yet, and yet, of all the great gaps that exist between holiday-brochure-world and holiday-reality-world, there is none so great as that in the caravanning experience.

The holiday sales-people love responding to questions, and I had a grand chat with one of them, details of which I now print here.

Times Square: Judging by the colour pics of the caravan "lounge" and its bedrooms, compared with their actual size, you are clearly in possession of a very rare wide-angle or fish-eye camera lens. In fact on entry to the wood-land caravan site, we presumed we had wandered into a settlement area for midgets – I beg your pardon, vertically challenged people. Anwyay, as a photographic enthusiast myself, can you tell me where I might obtain such a lens?

We regret to say this magnificent custom-made lens is not available to the general public but only to bona-fide caravan holiday marketing personnel.

I see. For measurement purposes, I took an average-size Irish cat with me and found I was unable to swing him in any room without causing the poor creature severe concussion. Have you any comment?

You were clearly in breach of French quarantine laws and should also be grateful we have not reported you to the ISPCA.

I was promised an "en-suite" bathroom with my "master bedroom". This boiled down in campsite reality to a connecting door between the sole loo-cum-shower and the "master bedroom", so-called presumably because of its masterly arrangement of bed, press and wardrobe, allowing entry and exit only by abstruse mathematical and geographical calculation. Don't you think your descriptions are a little on the flowery side?

Thank you. It is so nice to be complimented.

I don't wish to go on about the "bathroom", but would love to know one thing: where was the bath?

If you check any reputable dictionary you will find "bath" defined as a receptacle for bathing. Bathing in turn is defined as immersion of the body. This activity was perfectly possible in your bathroom.

On the contrary, the only immersion possible was in a vertical position, involving no more than about four inches of the lower leg, i.e. a little above the ankle. Is that your idea of a bath?

Please check your dictionary once again; you will find that immersion does not necessarily imply total immersion. We made no promise of in-caravan snorkelling facilities. Ha ha.

Ha ha. Now, if you opened the "bathroom" door in our caravan without warning, anyone standing in the "kitchen" (a corridor with a kettle) was liable to get a good whack in the ribs. If the second bedroom door was simultaneously opened, the potential for personal disaster was enormous. How did you come to design "family" caravans where one is a crowd?

By a process of trial and error. You seem to forget you were supposed to be out and about, and our caravans are designed to encourage you in such external and circuitous activity.

I can't begin to tell you how successful they are. But tell me this. Why is it that a caravan by its nature, always, without exception, has a permanently-dripping shower-head, or a dodgy shelf in the fridge, or a non-working cooker plate, or a door which won't close, or a jammed vent, or a combination of any or all of these?

These deliberate deficiencies come with our compliments and are meant to symbolise the pioneering spirt of adventurous living which has informed caravanning through the ages.

Thank you.

JAGGER STUNG BY UNSOLICITED TRIBUTES

Today being Mick Jagger's 50th birthday we have, to mark the event, secured an exclusive interview with Onan Only, one of the youngest of the estimated 394,578 pop pundits who have built a career on the Jagger/Rolling Stones "phenomenon".

Times Square: Onan, When you first appeared in print in *Way Out* magazine, writing about the early "wild excesses" of Mick Jagger, exactly what age were you?

Seven and a half.

Presumably then you did not know exactly what wild excesses were.

That's right. But I knew it sounded good. Or bad, which has more publicity value.

How right you were. But you probably know all about such excesses now?

Certainly not. You don't seem to appreciate the demands of this business. Most of us neither drink nor smoke. We didn't get to where we are now by frittering our time and health away in the sort of pursuits I presume you have in mind.

Please forgive me. You were also, I understand, the first pundit to use the phrase *enfant terrible* in connection with Jagger. Were you then an *enfant terrible* yourself?

I don't honestly know, to tell you the truth. What exactly does the phrase mean?

Oh, it hardly matters. I was just idly wondering if there was any way of stopping people using it now.

I'm afraid not. You see, it's a pretty well indispensable piece of shorthand for us in the pop business.

So tell me: how did you start to build up the Jagger image?

Well, basically I fed off the fantasies.

Jagger's?

God, no. Those of the punters. And of other pop pundits.

So it was a parasitic relationship?

I don't know. Have you got any better long word?

Symbiotic?

Yeah, I think I can handle that.

What it means is –

Forget it. It sounds fine.

Right. Now, you've written five books about Jagger. When did you first meet him?

Meet him? Why should I want to meet him? I wouldn't have time.

Quite. Let me bring you back a little. I recall that you spoke at length on prime-time TV about the "unspeakable horror" of the Altamont riots. You were very upset by these events?

Upset? Of course not. Why should I have been upset? You don't seem to appreciate the nature of show-business.

Probably not. But listen – is there any hope that if and when Jagger reaches the age of 60, the pop pundit industry will have found some new clichés to describe him then?

Frankly, I doubt it. Why coin new clichés when we have a set which has already stood the test of time?

I see what you mean. Onan, before I go any further I should warn you that only last week I physically assaulted a person who described Jagger as a "rock infidel". I then hit him again when he used the word "strut" in connection with Jagger's stage act, and kicked him in the stomach when he mentioned Jagger's "strange androgynous appeal". He got up and ran away, still jeering me and spewing grime-encrusted appellations like "ageing rocker" as he went. The Circuit Court judge (a contemporary of mine) later said he understood my feelings, and was imposing a fine only with great reluctance. Have you any comment to make?

You mean about Jagger, the pop phenomenon and sex icon whose songs symbolise sexual independence and emotional liberation, the archetypal bad boy and ultimate rebel and devil incarnate who strutted his way across the world stage from enfant terrible *of the permissive generation to pillar of the 1990s Establishment – help !!*

Thank you, goodbye and happy birthday Mick.

FUN CHILD LET LOOSE IN THE OFFICE

I was reading in this paper recently about a "laughter therapist" who is employed in that capacity by the West Birmingham Health Authority and who apparently teaches people to combat illness by releasing the "fun child" within them. "Set yourself a goal to do something bizarre, silly and/or eccentric at least once a week," he urges; "create an eccentrics' night out among friends or colleagues" and so on.

A few days later I read of a new book advising on how to achieve a "natural high", instead of depending on drink and other drugs. Natural highs apparently could be induced by climbing a mountain, laughing, cycling down a steep hill, daydreaming, eating jelly babies or listening to Daniel O'Donnell sing. Presumably one could even combine these, and achieve natural highs by climbing a mountain to get away from Daniel O'Donell, laughing at Daniel O'Donnell, cycling down a steep hill when Daniel O'Donnell has his back turned at the bottom, eating Daniel O'Donnell's jelly babies or simply not listening to Daniel O'Donnell sing. The opportunities are endless.

But there were some unanswered questions regarding both reports. Bizarre behaviour might well lower one's own blood pressure, but what might it do to other people's? And if you got "naturally high" on a regular basis, say – let us stretch a point – by listening to Daniel O'Donnell, surely you would run the risk of addiction? Can anyone imagine what it would be like to be addicted to Daniel's music? The secrecy, the shame, the broken families, the bingeing on tapes and CDs, the lost weekends. A support group would have to be set up – Danielaholics Anyonymous (Dan Anon), and so on.

But perhaps this is mere scaremongering. Scorning the cynics, I decided to embrace both theories, and achieve a natural high by releasing the fun child within me. The office seemed the natural place to start.

I began with a really comical, though perhaps not altogether original ploy. With my colleague briefly away from her desk, I left a message for her to phone "Mr Bear" and appended a phone number. Yes, you guessed it – she found herself put through to Dublin Zoo. Well, I laughed till I cried. You can imagine then how taken aback I was when she began screaming at me for wasting her time with my "inane jokes"; but I'm pretty sure, judging by the playful kick she landed in my groin, that she really was tremendously amused.

The next wheeze I came up with was sneaking a funny-happy message on to my boss's answerphone. This was a little piece of innocent fun combining a cheery greeting ("Hi there!") with a little bit of positive philosophy ("Have you made someone smile today?") and a rather good "knock-knock" joke.

To my disappointment however I gather that some of my boss's clients found it, to use his secretary's word, "infuriating". Clearly they have not yet released the fun children within them.

Anyway, with clients' calls apparently beginning to dry up completely, the boss has put up a notice offering a reward to whoever finds the "culprit" – me! I feel sure this is his own way of expressing his amusement, but modesty forbids me revealing my identity.

I felt so high at this stage I could almost see over the office partitions. But I didn't stop. No. I organised a hilarious gorillagram to mark our cleaner's 85th birthday (she is recovering quite well but still cannot receive visitors), pinned up the most amusing notices ("Tired of work? Then hold a meeting"!), switched the office tea and coffee containers and glued a "pretend" fifth-floor button in the lift. It was gratifying then that within a few weeks I was known throughout the building as the Office Joker, with some of the even wittier staff acclaiming me as the Office Clown.

As a particular highlight, I followed the laughter therapist's advice and organised an "Eccentrics' Night Out". There was enormous interest in the office, I took a lot of bookings, and planned a really wacky night. And guess what happened? Nobody turned up. All my colleagues had secretly got together to *pretend* they were going to go. Well of course I saw the funny side straight away; alone there in the community hall, I laughed myself sick. It was even more amusing when I came to work next day; I haven't seen so many fun children released in my colleagues for a long time.

Anyway I decided eventually that my own fun child was beginning to get a little out of hand, so I've locked it up within me again for another while. If it behaves itself, I might consider releasing it (on parole) in a few years' time.

LAST OF THE SMALLTIME SPENDERS

I was impressed with all the financial advice offered to the recent £3 million Lottery winner and, delighted with my own good fortune on the same day, an unexpected £2 scratch-card win, I decided to seek some professional investment advice myself.

I duly proceeded to Henshaw Ventures, an impressive downtown office with a smoked-glass door and a cut-glass secretary. Had I an appointment, enquired this magnificent creature? No, I admitted, but added, lowering my voice, that I was a Lottery winner. Straightway, some of the ice melted from the young woman's upper slopes. Moments later I was ushered into the inner sanctum of Henshaw himself, and I can tell you the milieu was a lot more impressive than that of my local credit union office.

Henshaw was an impressive bulk of thrusting middle-aged manhood in a three-piece suit. "So,"he said, tapping the desk with a wad of Giro transfers, "you're one of the anonymous Lottery winners?"

"I am."

"I believe in being blunt, Anon: how much have you to invest?"

"I'd rather not say at this point," I responded guardedly.

Henshaw laughed appreciatively: "Can't say I blame you."

"Indeed why should you?", I responded gaily.

Henshaw was delighted with me. He produced two massive cigars, chopped the ends off them with a marvellous little silver contraption and handed me one. I don't smoke, but didn't want to spoil Henshaw's happiness. The thing felt like a warm cucumber in my mouth. Henshaw then activated what appeared to be an army-issue flame-thrower. I drew on the cigar and leant back in the reclining leather-covered chair. When his secretary came in with champagne and a brand-new factory-fitted smile, and accidentally slipped me her private phone number while shaking hands, I could already feel the adrenalin of high finance.

Henshaw straightaway proposed that I have a "portfolio" of investments, with half my money in the bank, a quarter in stocks and shares and the rest in property.

I found the the word "portfolio" hugely attractive.

Henshaw eagerly pushed across his enormous ready reckoner and I began to tap in a few figures. My particular portfolio would, I calculated, be made up of one pound in the bank, drawing interest of perhaps 7p annually (before tax), 50p in stocks and shares and 50p in property. I must admit the gambling element of all this attracted me enormously.

"I wouldn't mind," I said lightly, "being a little more adventurous."

Henshaw was amazed and delighted. "I must say I wouldn't have thought that to look at you", he remarked candidly. "Just shows how wrong appearances can be."

I matched his loud, but oddly attractive guffaw with one of my own.

"Let me guess" said Henshaw through a cloud of grey smoke, "you're a wine buff, right?"

I thought about the last time, some six years back, I had invested in a half bottle of Mateus Rosé. There is still a little of it left, I believe.

"Keep a well-filled cellar, I'll bet?", went on Henshaw eagerly.

I marvelled at how the man could know of the windowless cell adjoining my basement flat. As far as I could recall, it housed the rusty remains of a bicycle, the motor unit of an old spin drier, and, if my land-lady has not been helping herself again, a bag and a half of coal.

"I might have some space to spare," I responded cautiously.

"Right," said Henshaw, grabbbing a pencil. "Let me suggest some vintage port – 50 cases to start?"

"Fifty cases," I mused.

"Done."

Henshaw went on to open up further exciting investment vistas in the worlds of fine art, antique toys, Bolivian tin miles and dwarf slave labour ventures in the Paraguayan rain forest. The man was possessed, his calculator jumping on the desk as his chubby fingers worked overtime.

"Enough,", I said finally: "You have convinced me." I stood up, took the two gleaming pound coins from my pocket and laid them reverently on Henshaw's desk.

"What are those?"

"My winnings."

"All of them?"

"Every last penny."

"And this is what you want me to invest for you?"

"It is."

Henshaw laid his head on the desk and began to cry. I was deeply moved: it is not often one sees an investment consultant show emotion in front of money, or indeed in front of anything. I know now my Lottery proceeds are in safe hands. And in the investment game, confidence is everything.

I'M SORRY TO HAVE TO BRING THIS UP

You might have seen where the Japanese Government recently made a formal apology to tens of thousands of women forced into serving its wartime soldiers as sex slaves. The apology came 48 years after the end of the second World War.

This raises the interesting question of when it is appropriate to apologise after offending someone. Immediately? Forty-eight years later? Somewhere in between? Is there an optimum cooling-off period for the offended party? If so, how can one know how long it should be? What form should an apology take? Or should one follow the adage, never apologise and never explain? Are there too many questions being posed here?

If so, sorry.

Presumably there are some crimes for which no apology could ever suffice, and others committed so long ago that apologies now seem pointless. Can one imagine picking up an east European newspaper, for example, and reading the following: "To the mothers-inlaw of my late ancestor, and their descendants, I would like to say, on great-great-great-great-greatuncle Bluebeard's behalf – a great big sorry." Or a personal notice in the *Palestine News:* "I wish to offer a belated but honest apology, and I am sure parents of small children will appreciate the nervous stress which caused my late ancestor, Herod, to behave the way he did." Or in the *Transylvania Times:* "It has come to my notice that a titled ancestor on my mother's side some centuries ago indulged in a truly shameful taste for the blood of young virgins. May I, on Count Dracula's behalf, say how truly sorry I am."

Love, of course, means always having to say you're sorry, and it is among the young married that the ludicrously embarrassing business of counter-apology is most pervasive. You know the kind of thing:

"I'm so sorry darling, it was all my fault." `

"No no, it was all mine."

"No, I insist, I'm entirely to blame."

And so on until the pair fall into each other's arms, conveniently forgetting that blame has not been properly allotted and the whole thing will be resurrected even more bitterly during the next row. Wouldn't it be better in the long run if one spouse said something like " Well actually darling, it *was* your fault, but I forgive you anyway"?

In the short run, of course, the most likely outcome would be murder.

If one accepts that apologies are best made as soon as possible, then why not take this theory to its natural conclusion and make them in advance?

What if a fellow were to beetle off to work one morning and, with the best of intentions, leave the following note:

"Darling, I'm so sorry. Today I have every intention of making a spur-of-the-moment decision to accompany the lads in the office on an almighty blow-out, starting in the nearest pub in the early afternoon and most likely culminating somewhere in the gutters of Leeson Street a good deal later. I confidently expect we shall all behave abominably, myself most of all, and it is unlikely you will see or hear from me before about five o'clock in the morning when I shall be trying to get the key in the door. I'm genuinely sorry about this and trust you will accept my sincere apologies. Yours regretfully."

This would be a lot more honest but do you think a spouse would find it more acceptable than a post-doghouse-exit apology the following week? You do? You're not married, I take it?

But there is surely nothing more outrageous than the death-bed apology. A fellow lies down to die after a life of unmitigated devilment – alcohol, women, cigarettes, cards, the lot. The mournful crowd, all long faces, gathers round, your man suddenly opens his eyes and blurts out something along the lines of "If there's anything at all I've done wrong..." Anything at all he's done wrong? Yet before you know it everyone is full of pathetic reassurances *They* are apologising to *him*. The corpse-to-be smiles beatifically and dies irretrievably forgiven. Those at his bedside weep tears of frustration and make secret plans to attend self-assertion courses.

Why do people tie themselves in knots like this? Sorry, I don't know, I apologise, didn't even mean to ask.

AVOID THOSE (PARENTAL) SCHOOLROOM BLUES

Now that a whole new generation of miniature adults has just entered our educational system, I am delighted to see that the INTO has published a booklet, *Your Child in the Primary School,* which gives useful practical information on everything from preparation for school to health and hygiene, from homework to parent-teacher communication. However, there remain some informational gaps, and it is with a view to filling these in that this column will shortly be issuing its complementary booklet, *Your Parent in the Primary School*, the main points of which are herewith summarised.

Preparation. Gently talk your parents through things for the first few days: they will need a lot of reassurance. Coming to terms with your schoolgoing status is difficult for most parents, and the aim is to gradually accustom them to the idea that you will no longer be with them for part of the day – and that it really won't be very long before you have nothing more to do with them. As they grow older you will be pleased to see them accepting this prospect more philosophically.

It is also a very good idea to bring your parents along to the school and acquaint them with your new environment, allowing them to gush as much as they like over its attractions. It's embarrassing for you, of course, but just remember that all children suffer equally.

The First Few Days. Your parents will naturally be nervous at handing over their cherished caring role to a complete stranger, so watch for signs of imminent tears or even total breakdown, and move quickly to control the situation. While the handover from parent to teacher is crucial, staying around is not a good idea. So go straight to your desk. Your parents will probably hang about the gate making quite heartbreaking small talk with other anguished parents but will eventually go away. Do not prolong the agony by waving to them.

General Appearance. Never mind what other children tell you: appearances *do* matter, and it is important that your parents should create a good impression and embarrass you as little as possible on arrival at your school. Kick up an almighty fuss if they affect the trendy young parent look, and be similarly strict if they show signs of believing that scruffiness is somehow "cool".

Bullying. This is a notoriously tricky area in many schools, and difficult to root out, as it rarely takes a physical form. Some parents are more susceptible than others – there is undoubtedly an element of masochism – and find themselves involved in far too many school runs, extra-curricular duties, school play activities and so on. You will have to keep a very close eye on your own parents, your friends' parents – and your teachers.

Child collection. In the initial weeks, you should try to make a big fuss when your parents arrive to pick you up, and then gradually ease off on the histrionics. If your parents are late collecting you, particularly in these first few weeks, admonish them firmly but don't upset them too much. Every year there are tearful scenes with parents breaking down simply because they arrive a few minutes late. You must help them to get things in perspective.

Helping at Home. Be gentle but firm when your parents offer to help you with homework. Let them help, but not too much. You will also need to be sensitive when they make errors.

Attitude problems. If you already have siblings at school, you may well notice a certain parental casualness creeping in regarding your own attendance. You must nip this nonchalance in the bud. You are at least as important as your brothers and sisters, so make sure your parents recognise the fact. And while it is quite acceptable to have your parents patronise you, no nonsense is to be tolerated from the rest of the family.

Making Friends. our mum and dad will be nervous for a while as they gradually get to know other parents. Encourage them to be sociable and show them how easy it can be, and what fun, to make new friends. But recognise that as adults they are very much set in their ways.

Independence. It is always a tricky time when parents are taking their first faltering steps towards child-free life. You will want to be supportive, but not overtly so. Use the common sense with which your four or five years have amply provided you.

A DEDICATED FOLLOWER OF FASHION PROSE

Forever fascinated by fashion, I was greatly taken by the piece in this paper 0last week about young British tailor Ozwald Boateng, apparently the hippest guy to go to these days if you desire, as which of us doesn't, to be at the cutting edge of fashion, particularly when it comes to a decent suit.

The article made me realise that the autumn season was already well into its stride, so prior to checking out the boutiques I decided I should follow the preliminary advice of all the very best fashion commentators, and take a long hard look at my wardrobe.

It's quite a while since I did this, but the experience was as absorbing as ever. My wardrobe is of those solid constructions from the 1950s, and the watermarks and scratches on its mahogany doors detract surprisingly little from its serene beauty. It is a wardrobe of considerable character.

In the end, however, after a really long hard look, I have to admit I got bored. So I opened the wardrobe. Checking the standard fashion advice column, I now realised I had "hard decisions" to make. Furthermore, my approach should be "ruthless". Basically, I had to throw out anything over two years old, plus any item I had not worn in the last season.

I went to work. When I had finished my wardrobe was quite empty, apart from some old Bulgarian coins and an unfinished chocolate bar lurking in a corner. All of these being clearly over the two-year mark, I threw them out too.

I now had to go shopping for some new gear, a suit being the most urgent priority. So I rang Ozwald Boateng at the London number thoughtfully provided by *The Irish Times* article, and got his secretary, who offered me an appointment in early December. I then asked politely about the costs, asking her to be quick, as the sand in my three-minute timer was running out. Inexplicably, she straight away told me I couldn't afford "a Boateng" and hung up.

A mite rueful, I went back to Joe, my tailor for forty-oddd years, who still works in his little lean-to off Clanbrasil Street. When I got there I felt guilty for even thinking of deserting him for Boateng.

"Is it 1993 already? Same again I suppose?" asked Joe, reaching for his tape-measure.

"Well, not quite,"I ventured. "You are no doubt aware, Joe, that the new lean-look suit has emphatically ousted the baggy tailoring of the 1980s?"

Joe showed no reaction, other than dropping his tape-measure, so I continued: "And that with regard to the masculine leg, the finesse of its turn and the elongated langour of its gait are employed to the greatest advantage under stove-pipe trousers and those high-waisted jackets which upholster every nuance of the pectorals?"

"Who told you that?"

"The *Irish Times.*"

Joe pulled out a roll of dark tweed. "This do you?"

I inspected the tweed. It was little different from the material he had used to make my last five suits.

"You don't happen to have any Wain & Sheil swatches, do you? Nothing in wild slub silk? Or crushed organza? No. Well, it *may* do," I went on, "but I will need a guarantee."

"A guarantee?"

"That the cut and materials will metamorphose a standard suit into a sexy, second shell. That the lean lines will cleave closer to the body than a Lycra catsuit, that the shoulders are cut flashily wide to enhance the iron-pumped brawn. Further, that the trousers are vacuum-packed around long, long legs, that a protective aura of androgyny will be created and that there will at length emerge from your studio a velveted daddylong-legged dandy. After all, I ask only that you do what Mr Ozwald Boateng can apparently do, and deliver on the promise of *Irish Times* prose."

Joe took a look around the lean-to. "Iron-pumped brawn," he mused. "A sexy second shell. Who do you want this suit for?"

"Joe, it's like this. Amid the hyperactive clones in ubiquitous baggy and logo-ed sportswear, I have decided to internationalise the worthy crusade by Ozwald Boateng to highlight good bodies in the nattiest tailoring, and bring suave back to the streets of Ireland's capital."

Joe had the grace to wish me good luck, before slamming the door. Sadly, Joe no longer speaks the language of fashion, but he is literate enough in his own way.

THE PERILS OF PLAIN COOKING

I was almost in tears after reading the recent interview in *The* (London) *Independent* with renowned chef Anton Mosimann. As proprietor of his own Belgravia dining club, where members rarely pay less than £100 for dinner, Anton clearly has it made. But that does not prevent him suffering the agonies peculiar to his art: "We are in a creative position where what we create is gone the next moment. A painting, a house, a room stays for life. In our case it's just the opposite. We have to create again and again. One day you want to cry out of happiness at what you've achieved but the following day you have to do it again, constantly reaching for perfection."

Anton is right. The home, as he remarks, stays for life (though I would like Anton's opinion on my sagging roof), but the dinner has to be made every day.

Delighted to find someone so in tune with my own outlook, I was eager to learn more from the eminent chef. So I took careful note of his advice to other cooks: "Don't try to overdo things or use too many ingredients. Leave the taste of what it is. Chicken should taste like chicken and fish like fish. That's vital. So many people try to overpower good produce, for example with alcohol. Leave it plain. That's healthy too, and to take care of people's health and wellbeing is part of my responsibility."

Could anything be clearer? It suddenly dawned on me what terrible mistakes I had been making.

It was true that my few of my dinner guests had been heard complaining before, except on the infamously embarrassing night the 28th and final bottle of *vin rouge ordinaire* ran out. But obviously it was out of politeness that they had eaten up even my most exotic creations, confections full of liquor and cream and other health-threatening ingredients. How many dishes had I overpowered with alcohol, without a word of complaint? I was embarrassed to think of how thoughtful and patient my guests had always been, despite what they must have been suffering.

At my next dinner party, I resolved that things would be different. After all, if Anton doesn't know about food, then who does?

On the night, I began with *chicken chinoise à la soy sauce*. In keeping with Anton's advice, it was a simple dish. Basically, it was boiled chicken which just sat there, in extremely small pieces, with a tangential blob of soy sauce. My guests sampled it. Indeed, in the act of sampling it, they polished it off. They looked disappointed. How did it taste, I asked them? Like chicken, they admitted a little shamefacedly. I told them it *was* chicken. They shrugged their shoulders, collectively.

I served the main course. "What's this," said one guest humorously, "Roast-lamb-with-nothing-done-to-it?"

I felt the need to explain. So I told them what Anton said about simplicity. About keeping things plain. About responsibility for one's guests' health and wellbeing. About overpowering things with alcohol and the like.

My oratory, and Anton's opinions, were lost on them. I never saw people look so glum.

There was silence, then my guests began reminiscing about some of the "great" meals they had once had in my house, before I discovered simple cooking. "Chicken that tastes like chicken," one of them was repeating sadly – "What's the point of that?" His face looked like a collapsed soufflé.

Back in the kitchen, I realised my simple dessert of vanilla ice-cream, tasting like vanilla ice-cream, was clearly destined to fail. So I roused myself. I took the ice-cream and doused it in gin. I emptied a box of mint chocolate chips on top, added half a pint of Arabian orange liqueur and some icing sugar, then wrapped the whole thing in readymade pancakes. I whipped up some double cream and flavoured it with a dash of Drambuie; plus dashes of Bailey's Cream, Power's whiskey, Four Seasons bourbon, Stolichnaya vodka and green Chartreuse. I poured it over.

Without ceremony, I carried the whole thing to the table and put a match to it. Blue and green flames shot up to the ceiling. There were gasps of astonished delight, then silence. Sampling began: the stuff disappeared down eager throats and the compliments flowed as fast as the wine. Nobody mentioned the word ice-cream, and you never saw people so happy.

Sadly, it has become clear to me that my guests do not possess palates as educated as those of Anton's. Maybe if I charged them £100 a throw, they might learn to appreciate a little simplicity. But I doubt it.

HERE'S ONE I PREPARED EARLIER

Good evening and welcome to the Politically Correct Cookery Programme. Yes, this wonderful business of political correctness, whereby one is ever so careful not to insult any person, place or thing, any beliefs, feelings, or opinions – however daft – has even infiltrated the domain of TV cookery programmes. Hard to credit, but nonetheless true.

Let us call our typical TV cook Harriet. She is demonstrating how to prepare for example, fried chicken breasts in a wine and tarragon sauce. Fine. But straightaway, Harriet is attacked by the PC virus. She suddenly realises that not everyone will be able to afford, or have access to, all the ingredients. So the patter changes, nervously: "Now, take your chicken. If you haven't got a chicken, rabbit is really just as nice. . ."

Harriet pauses again. "It may be, of course, that you may not have a rabbit either." Harriet frowns, then brightens. "If not, then take six eggs. Well, perhaps one will do."

All over the country, amateur cooks in their kitchens are waiting, chickens, rabbits and egg(s) at the ready. And Harriet carries on. "Now, place your dish on the gas ring." Harriet pauses, frowns, brightens again. "Of course, if you haven't got a gas ring, simply light a small fire on the floor. And if you haven't got a dish..."

And so on. "And there we are. Fried chicken breasts in a wine and tarragon sauce. All on a bed of chicory leaves." Or in your case, burnt rabbit legs in an extremely thin cider and dandelion sauce, on a bed of cabbage. And in someone else's case, parboiled egg in water and nettle gravy, on a bed of fresh grass.

Daft, what? Anyway, it has occurred to me that in the event of this column not appearing for some reason or other, you would appreciate having the recipe to hand, so that you can run up one of your own. So here it is. Cut it out and keep in a safe place.

First, grab a handful of newspapers and scour for suitably offbeat news items, or comments. You will rarely find any, but never mind. Lay the papers out across your desk, with items dramatically marked in bright red or yellow highlighter. Depending on which boss you need to impress, aim for a look of controlled but urgent chaos. Scribble two or three "while you were out" messages to yourself and stick them on your monitor. Then nip across to Bewley's. If there is no Bewley's near you, any coffeehouse will do. So too will any pub, but it is not really a good idea. Not yet, anyway.

When you return, ask if your muse has called. Laugh, because no one else will. Then rearrange your desk and go walkabout in the office.

As a "humorous" writer, you will find yourself regularly being stopped and told jokes. As far as your piece for the paper goes, they will all be quite unusable, and very often, if you work in this office, unprintable.

Go back to your desk and repeat the best and/or longest of the bad jokes you have heard to your nearest colleague, preferably if he/she is absorbed in work. It will often turn out that your colleague has initiated the particular joke, and is not amused at the interruption. Never mind. You have disturbed a logical thought process, and this is the essence of your work.

Go and have a long lunch. Time will be running out when you return, but stay calm. Go direct to your screen. Take your selected news story. Twist it inside out. Nip out to the herb garden and pick some fresh wit (dry or sparkling): remove its soul, commonly known as brevity, and mix in. Add a dash of sarcasm and wit, plus a pun or two for flavour. Season with flair and imagination, or failing that, anything you can find in your larder.

Leave everything to simmer. Meanwhile make a rich sauce of commentary and observation, whipping it until it stands up in peaks. Do not allow to curdle. Pour over and serve.

PROSE AND CONS OF A WRITING CAREER

I was intrigued by a piece in *The Daily Telegraph* recently about the lot of the serious novelist in today's society, an article which featured various writers moaning about misunderstanding and lack of appreciation.

"There's a sort of post-Thatcherite thing that you ought to be doing an airport book with a plot to earn your keep," complained Emma Tennant. "The 'serious' novelist is perceived as a waste of time and money. The novel has become the Fergie of the literary world."

"I'm just sick and tired of the whole business," groaned Alice Thomas Ellis.

"When I was a child I read books because I enjoyed them, not because I was interested in the people who wrote them. Now novelists are expected to be public figures, popping up on television the whole time."

As a serious, though unpublished, novelist myself, I found myself greatly perturbed at all of this. So before committing myself finally to the career of author, I went along to talk to the distinguished writer Jonathan Ashton Thimbleby- Khart, in his modest riverside manor.

I sought out Thimbleby-Khart because he has seen just about every side of writing life. As readers may recall, he began his professional career as a *belletrist*. He then flourished briefly as a poet, published and unpublished, in that order. Next he wrote a *novella* or two, and later became a biographer of little-known 17th century poets.

During all of this time, he told me, he was ecstatically happy. He had enough to live on and no one bothered him. No one asked him for opinions, invited him to conferences, sought autographs or disturbed him in any way because of his occupation.

"Then I made a terrible mistake: I decided to become a serious novelist. It was all foolish pride, of course, and you know what pride precedes. I saw the warning signs very quickly, because straight away I began to get favourable reviews, and my sales began to soar. I began to write less and less, keeping my third book down to a mere 63 pages, hoping it might escape notice, but the heavyweight newspaper reviewers jumped on it ecstatically. Desperate, I reduced my works to mere paragraphs, and eventually mere sentences. All it did was increase my fame. But the last straw was the series of chat shows."

"You were a disaster?"

"No, I was a huge success. The public, you see, can't get enough of taciturn individuals like myself – a psychologist told me it's because they're sick of media personalities endlessly rabbiting on and on. But I couldn't stand all the public appearances or the pronouncements I was expected to make on world affairs, of which I understand next to nothing. My problem was that no one would take me frivolously."

Thimbleby-Khart shook his head sadly and tugged on a tapestry bell-pull. A young woman dressed in a Roman toga appeared and served champagne. "In the end," he went on, "I'm afraid I just had to assert myself and make the break: so I became a pulp writer of romantic prose."

"You succumbed to that post-Thatcherite thing that Emma Tennant spoke of?" "Well, Emma has the wrong end of the literary stick. My decision had nothing to do with earning my keep. It was simply the only way to retain my sanity. I decided to start with an airport book, and my first effort was *A History of Heathrow*. Gratifyingly, this sold only seven copies, so I followed it up with *Gate Choice at De Gaulle*, *The Kennedy Carousels* and *All You Ever Wanted to Know About Luton*. But my publisher then stepped in to give me a few pointers, and you know what followed."

"Fame and fortune?"

"Good God, no. A respectable but hardly extraordinary income, but more importantly, a decent level of obscurity. No one, as you know, reviews pulp fiction."

"So you don't have people bothering you all the time, then?"

"Certainly not. You're the first for years. And you're going now, aren't you?

"Yes. Thank you."

"Thank *you* and goodbye."

HIT AND MYTH AT THE THEATRE FESTIVAL

One of the great unpublicised scandals of this year's Dublin Theatre Festival has been the Abbey's out-of-hand rejection of a ground-breaking new work by young Ballydehob-based playwright Laetitia van der Hoostenhaus. *Leda an' de Swan* is her deeply moving and delightfully vernacular transposition of the ancient Greek myth to a modern Irish setting, and the scene below, which Laetitia has kindly allowed me to transcribe, will give some flavour of what Dublin audiences have missed.

The scene: inner-city Dublin flat. Enter 14-year-old Leda, dripping wet, to be greeted by her mother.

The Ma: So dere y'are. Where wurr ye for de last tree hours?

Leda: Juss down be de river, Ma.

The Ma: Well yer dinner's cold – ah Jaysus, looka de state-a-ye! Whah happened?

Leda: Nuttin, Ma.

The Ma: Come on, ouh widdit. Mudderagod, yer soakin!

Leda breaks down crying.

Leda: I have sumpin to tell ye, Ma – I got tooken advantage of!

The Ma: Whah?

Leda: Down be the river, Ma.

The Ma: Never mind where. The ting is, who? Who wazza?

Leda bawls again.

Leda: It wazza swan, ma!

Long pause.

The Ma: A swan. Jaysus Leda luv, yer in a bad way. I'll get some towels.

Leda: Fekk the towels, ma – I'm serious! It wazza swan!

The Ma: A swan?

(The Ma moves threateningly towards Leda)

Lissen Leda, don't wind me up. I'm not in de humour.

Leda: I'm tellin ye de trute! I wudden lie abou sumpin like dis!

The Ma: A swan. Ye were tooken advantage of be a –

Leda: *(losing patience)* Yea, yea, a swan, a great big shaggin swan! He juss jumped me, whah could I do?

The Ma: *(lights fag nervously)* Ah jaysus, wait'll yer da hears dis news.

Leda: Ah ma – don't tellim – he'll murder me!

The Ma: Here he comes now, ye can tellim yerself.

Enter the Da, walking just a bit erratically.

The Da: How're yiz? Juss in time for de dinner, am I? Nice timin', wha?

The Ma: Leda has sumpin to tell ye, Anto.

Leda: Ah Ma!

The Da: Whah izza? Jaysus, were ye swimmin, Leda? Could ye not wait t'get yer togs on or wha?

The Da falls about in a fit of laughing, which abruptly changes to coughing. He sits down heavily.

The Ma: Will ye shut up Anto, ye stewpid eejah. Ye won't be laffin when ye hear the news.

The Da: So tellus? Leda, what's up?

Leda: Me, da. I'm up de pole. Sorry Da.

The Da: Oh. Righ. So whose izza?

Leda: One o' dem swans down be de river, Da.

The Da: *(thoughtfully)* Is dat righ? Y'know, I always said some o' dem lads had a gamey eye.

The Ma: Anto! Did ye not hear what de young wan's after telling ye? She got tooken advantage of be a fekkin swan!

The Da: Ma, will ye shut up a minnit. Listen, Leda: ye needn't worry, I'm not goin to hit ye. Juss tell me de wan thing.

Leda: Wha, da?

The Da: Tell me the trute now: did ye lead him on?

Leda: Ah Da!

The Da: Awrigh, awrigh. Dat's fine. Dese tings happen, ye know. It's only nattchurel.

The Ma: Nattchurel! Anto! A great big bleedin swan!

The Da: Don't worry yerself now, Leda. An annuder ting *(The Da scratches his ear thoughtfully)* I remember hearin dat swans does make very good fadders.

Leda starts bawling again.

The Ma: Ah fer jaysus sake Anto – what I wanta know is, whattye goin to do abourra? Can we sue de Corpo or whah?

The Da: Do? I'm goin down to de Anchor for a few scoops, dat's what I'm doin fer starters. Jaysus, it's not every day a fella hears he's goin to be a granda, wha?

The Ma: No. Not a granda of bleedin' cygginets anyway, ye fekkin eejah!

Exit the Da. Door slams. Curtain falls.

PASSIVE SEX HEALTH HAZARD SHOCK

With the Irish public only beginning to come to terms with recent revelations on passive smoking, shock findings have just been published on the controversial subject of passive sex which, according to new figures is now thought to wear out 81,387 people annually in this country alone. The findings, published by the Institute for New Things To Worry About, are expected to provide a new stimulus in the campaign to outlaw sex activism in the workplace.

Moreover, the report also stresses the hazards of "environmental sex" – e.g. in posters, pictures of Naomi Campbell, films, magazines, pictures of Naomi Campbell, newspapers, the proliferation of "better sex" videos and pictures of Naomi Campbell. In the words of institute director Klefstein A Murphy, "this thing is all around us; something has to be done."

Publication of the findings was welcomed by Professor Stefan G Fotherington of the Campaign for Stopping All This, who insists that "other people's sex lives, and pictures of Naomi Campbell, are not just a nuisance, but a health hazard too". In support of his claim he points out that over the past few years, hospital admissions for heavy breathing and breathlessness problems have soared, while the age profile of those being admitted to homes for the completely clapped-out has descended rapidly.

These findings will come as a relief to all those people who hitherto could get no medical advice or explanation for their problem of low energy level and regular feelings of exhaustion, satiety and, most distressing of all, complete boredom.

Times Square talked to one such victim, asking about his problems, how he dealt with them, and his reaction to the new findings.

TS: You were feeling run down, tired out, and were constantly falling asleep at your desk?

Victim: Yes.

TS: Tell me, do you have regular sex?

Victim: How dare you? I'm a married man.

TS: So you're a victim of passive sex.

Victim: Yes, I suffer the side effects of other people's activities.

TS: So how do you feel now about sex activists?

Victim: If they want to indulge their disgusting habit they should do it somewhere else.Otherwise they should be locked up.

TS: Isn't that going a little far?

Victim: They go all the way, why can't I?

TS: "Go all the way?" You were born in the fifties, were you?

Victim: Yes, what's that got to do with it?

TS: Never mind. What about Naomi Campbell pictures?

Victim: Please don't mention them, it brings on my migraine. Do you know, I'm more familiar with her body than my own? Can you imagine what sort of neurosis that causes?

TS: I'd rather not.

At this stage the victim had to lie down for a while.

Meanwhile a test case is already under way in the High Court. Mr. Wilfrid Cuthbertson-Wall, who describes himself ironically as an "old-age pensioner in my thirties", is suing his employers, Wonder Widgets Ltd, for health problems he alleges have resulted from his firm's "reckless" policy on sex in the workplace. Mr Cuthbertson-Wall wants the firm to set aside a room for sex activists and Campbell picture deviants, and to offer a sex cessation programme for those employees who want to get rid of their habit.

The company rejects the allegations and warns of the employment consequences should the case succeed: "If things go on like this, there won't be anyone left to work," said the angry manger of Wonder Widgets.

The multinational Naomi Campbell Picture Industry Incorporated has also hit back at the findings, urging the public to support continued saturation usage of its products in order to protect the jobs of 86,946 odd (sic) beneficiaries of the industry. These include, as it points out, Ms Campbell herself, her supporters, her minders, her friends; the *paparazzi* (and their families) and their assistants (and their families); plus newspaper and magazine employees around the world (and their families). The associate company, Naomi Campbell Useless Repetitive Droning Gossip Incorporated, has also urged support, citing the 58,765 odd (sic) social columnists, chat-show hosts, and sundry support staff (and their families) who depend on the business worldwide.

BOOM TIMES IN THE CELEB BIOG BUSINESS

I was intrigued by a report on the latest showbusiness biography, *The Secret Life of Bob Hope,* which apparently tells how the comedian traded girlfriends with Bing Crosby as part of an active extra-marital sex life, kept female companions in apartments near his California home and "made love to more beautiful women than Errol Flynn, Chico Marx and Bing Crosby combined".

By sheer coincidence, I read this report on the very day I myself applied for a job with Celebrity Biographers Ltd., who are enjoying boom times in the industry.

I was introduced straight away to executive vice-president Max J Schlingsummer, a small thin gentleman with an unusually sweaty forehead.

"Call me Max," said Max, pumping my hand furiously.

I undid a large folder containing my writing pedigree and CV, but Max put it aside after a casual glance.

"Tell me," he said, leaning back in his chair, "you ever done any fiction?"

I was pleased to reply that I dealt only in factual material.

Max didn't seem too impressed. "Facts are okay, kid, but the reading public gets kinda bored with 'em. Know what I mean? We're talking celeb biography here. Ya gotta use some imagination. So tell me, what kinda guys you biographed?"

I mentioned a couple of 17th-century philosophers and a rather obscure Victorian lepidopterist.

"Lepidopterist?" Max's tiny eyes lit up. "*Freaky.* Say, I've heard of a lot of kinky stuff but never *that* before. Still, life's a sewer and we can only keep swimmin', right? Lep*idopt*erist. No, don't tell me, I don't even want to think about it. Jeez, were those Victorians repressed or *what*."

Max's interest in me had clearly grown. "Say,"he went on, "what do you know about sexual impotence? You know, the old can't-get-it-up blues?"

"Nothing," I answered, taken aback."Without meaning to boast, you understand." I essayed a little laugh.

Max looked at me sadly. "Nothing at all? About impotence and the stars?"

I told him I hadn't realised there was an astrological influence.

"That's not what I meant," he said. "But never mind. How about wife-swapping in the movie business?"

I had to admit my ignorance. I knew one (weakish) joke on the subject but didn't think it wise to bring it up.

Max went on to inquire how well I was informed regarding the palimony situation in the US, the communications networks of international vice rings, the miscegenation laws in Kuala Lumpur, the logistics of five-in-a-bed "romps", the optimum duration of drink-drugs-and-sex binges, the fulfilment of bimbo quota requirements on the Costa Smeralda and the nocturnal entertainment facilities on Bend Street, Bangkok, with particular reference to group celebrity discounts.

Again I had to confess complete ignorance on all these subjects.

Max shook his head glumly. "Thought you said you were a facts man? For a would-be celeb biographer, you got some serious education gaps."

He was silent a moment, then perked up: "Tell you what, take Rick K. We're planning his bio. Now, do you figure Rick has slept with more women than, say, Groucho Marx or Douglas Fairbanks Jnr? Or would you say less than Burt Reynolds and Maurice Chevalier together?"

I thought about this until I was dizzy. "It's hard to say," I managed finally.

Max nodded understandingly. "Yeah, innit a bitch? Tell you the truth, math was never my strong point either. Look, here's a bunch of screwing-around figures. You work 'em out for me. Can you do that?"

Max threw me a calculator and a print-out. I did some quick sums and came up with a few figures.

Max was delighted: "Say, maybe you do have some biographical skills after all. So, lemme see: Rick got it over more than Chevalier and Reynolds separately, but less than Marx and Fairbanks together. Now, how about if we factor in Barbara Stanwyck, Gene Autry, Buster Keaton and Clara Bow?"

I keyed in the figures. Then I confirmed to Max that Rick succeeded with more women than either Autry or Keaton, and his tally came to exactly the number of men Bow and Stanwyck enjoyed *between* them.

Max was ecstatic. "Is this gonna make one hell of a biography or what?" He stuck out a bony paw. "You're hired."

"I'm a researcher, then?"

"A checker? Hell, no, they come two a penny. We're making you a vice-president in our Comparative Leg-over Enumeration Division. You got a future here, kid."

IS THERE A VACUUM IN *YOUR* MARRIED LIFE?

I was reading one of those newspaper agony aunt columns recently, as one tends to when the Booker Prize excitement is fading, and came across a letter from a newly-married woman who had come home unexpectedly one afternoon to find her husband hoovering the house in her silk slip and French knickers. The woman's first reaction was shock, then amusement. But having talked the matter over, the husband's explanations were apparently satisfactory, and the couple remained "blissfully happy". Yet the wife expressed a lingering concern about the future. Was it just a phase he was going through? Should she take action or would he get fed up with it anyway? Was he doing it "just as a novelty"?

I don't normally answer other people's letters, and the agony aunt certainly imparted some very useful advice: I would merely hope to give a man's point of view.

What you have to think about, my dear woman, is *why* you hope this is merely a phase your husband is going through. What frightens or upsets you about the idea that your husband might want to go on hoovering? Is it the idea that it may be less an amusement than a compulsion? Do you regard it as abnormal? Are you worried about what people might think?

At the moment, you and your husband are acting as though this is just an elaborate game. But I think your husband is being less than honest with you, and you are deliberately not asking him too many questions. In other words, the two of you are afraid to discuss what's actually going on here.

Your husband is probably one of the thousands, if not the hundreds of thousands, of men in Ireland who like hoovering. As you have discovered, it doesn't affect your sex life. On the contrary, it may well improve it. And your husband is still the man you love very much. He just happens to like hoovering.

Perhaps he indulges only now and again? Or is it possible that he harbours a secret desire to hoover all day long? You haven't said what excuse *he* had for being at home in the afternoon. You see, men vary widely in their desire to hoover. It doesn't mean they are less manly; it doesn't mean they are homosexual. What your husband will probably tell you when you get around to talking about it, is that hoovering simply relaxes him.

Your husband is very lucky. You have not only kept calm in the face of your discovery, but you have built his desire to hoover into your lives. If he goes on with it, however, you may have to urge him to be discreet. That way, you need not be nervous when visitors call or, later on, if you have children of your own.

Would I be correct in surmising that your household hoover was a wedding present? Can you remember who gave it to you? I have no desire to cause you unnecessary worry, but if the donor was male, it may well be that he is involved with your husband in a secret hoovering club. This is not necessarily a bad thing, but it might be worth looking into.

Finally, a few words of technical advice. If you are truly serious about accepting your husband for what he is, you should try to invest in the best hoover available. Why not go shopping together some day? My own personal recommendation would be an upright model with a motor operating on not less than 1,000 watts. Ideally too, the hoover you purchase should have all of the following: variable power, multilevel filtration, bag check indicator, brush height adjustment – and integral tools. *Nothing* is more frustrating than being poised to tackle those challenging little nooks and crannies and then discovering that the plastic clip-on thingy is still in the kitchen cupboard. Any man will tell you that.

You might also want to consider added suction power and the option of a spill pick-up tool. Easy conversion to shampooing mode is another useful feature on some models. All these embellishments will enhance your husband's pleasure and should ensure that your marriage remains as blissful as ever.

You have coped well with a potentially disastrous trauma: what you've learned is that your husband's behaviour doesn't hurt your relationship. On the contrary, it has brought you closer together. So don't worry about the future. Just keep those lines of communication open, and make sure your house always contains a good stock of hoover bags.

LOWERING THE TONE IN THE GYM

The British royals were in the news again when secretly-taken photographs of Princess Diana working out in a gym were published in one of the tabloids.

The London fitness club where the Princess Diana "peeping Tom" photographs were taken has received a number of angry phone calls from its members, and there have even been resignations. – *Newspaper report.*

Feelings were running high when I visited the exclusive and newly-famous fitness club in West London earlier this week, and I immediately sensed that the tension was not all due to the level of physical exertion on display. I had already heard stories of terrible scenes in the club on the day the Diana pictures were published. Some members had apparently been unable to contain their outrage, and one ruined a perfectly good pair of Ryka runners when kicking a Trotter treadmill, while another vandalised a brand-new Cibex leg press.

Fitness enthusiasts were furiously pumping iron and the aerobics floor was throbbing as I began my investigations by talking to, or rather, listening to Anemone Huntingdon-Lee, a voluptuous brunette in her mid-forties. Turning down the volume on *You're The One That I Want,* Anemone professed herself absolutely outraged at the Diana scandal. Spotjogging as she talked, she pointed out that she herself had been a member for five years and was in tip-top condition, which indeed was obvious. "Now, on the day the pictures were taken, I was wearing a hand-stitched silk Avia leotard in jade green, new allwhite Nike runners and candy-striped dayglo LA Gear cycling shorts purchased in Russell Square only three days previously".

"You must have looked terrific," I said politely.

"Well of course I did", responded Anemone brusquely, "I looked perfectly stunning. Five people remarked the fact to me and, I was propositioned three times, once successfully, before 11 a.m. And yet, you will hardly credit this, not a single photograph of me was released to the Mirror Group, though I understand some are in private circulation. Why should it always be Di whose privacy is invaded? When will the rest of us get a turn?"

I shook my head in silent commisseration as Anemone spun on a perfectly-sculpted heel and strode off to pulverize a padded leather pillow on her personal Fassi physique-builder.

Turning round, I bumped into a solid tree-trunk about eight feet high, which introduced itself to me as Sandy Whitby-Sandringham. Pumping my hand vigorously, Sandy returned it with no more than a couple of minor fractures and asked me to wait a few moments while he intimidated a Furschvaal toning machine.

Sandy had clearly long ago worked off not just all his excess body fat, but also his excess neck and waist, and now appeared intent on working off his excess legs as far up as the knee. He was wearing an undersized Asics string vest with holes the size of the Koh-i-noor Diamond, and black silk Lacoste shorts whose brevity, I thought, drew perhaps more attention than was necessary to the pelivc toning exercises in which he was simultaneously engaged.

"Bloody disgraceful," was Sandy's comment on the Diana affair when he took a short break. About two pints of sweat from his arm-pits spurted angrily over my shirt-front as he carried on. "Bloody embarrassing for her to have pics like that put out. Poor woman's metacarpals just halfway through the re-grinding process you know. Obvious for all to see. Rotten luck for her. All wrong. Caddish behaviour."

Sandy cranked his machine up into the red sector and I left him there, professionally bursting small blood vessels, while I moved on.

Over in a corner I found a slight young man, Rupert, mildly abusing a Climbax stepper. Rupert straightaway informed me, indeed without my asking, that he was an unemployed suspender-belt design consultant living with his friend Lance in a tiny Chelsea duplex on a small allowance of £100,000 p.a. from his estranged father, Lord Percival Grantham. He was absolutely distraught at not having had his picture used in the Mirror.

"Can you imagine," he whimpered, "what the publicity would have meant for my consultancy?"

I tried to, then gave up: "But what about the invasion of your privacy?"

"Gosh,"giggled Rupert, tugging out a lace-edged hankie from inside his peach-tinted Gilda Marx organza leotard and dabbing his forehead, "I should have thought that would be the most enjoyable aspect."

So how did he feel about the Diana pics? "Now you'll really get my blood up. Never gave the poor girl a chance to do her eyes. *Sooo* unfair". Rupert stamped his small Reebok-shoed foot in anger, then left his stepper for a session on the Greschen-Kvass eyebrow-flexer. Declining his kind offer to help with my toe cuticle alignment and improve my navel definition, I made my excuses and left.

FROM OUR WORLD CUP CORRESPONDENT

In November 1993, World Cup mania was beginning to sweep the nation...

Dear Auntie Lettie,

I'll bet you get a big surprise when you see the name at the bottom of *this* letter! But I'm sure you won't mind me calling you "Auntie", though of course I realise you were only married for nine weeks to my father's third cousin once removed.

Anyway, you're probably wondering why I'm writing, not having seen me since you visited the old sod when I was three days old. That's neither today nor yesterday! Well, it's like this: have you heard about something called the "World Cup"? I'm sure you Americans are just as excited about it as we are. And the great news is, Ireland are through to the finals! The Republic, I mean, not that shower of Prods over the Border, who nearly screwed the whole thing up for us.

So anyway – this is the really exciting bit – Chrissy and meself and Granny and the kids, who have been following the lads all along, are planning to hit the old US of A next summer, which is where you come in, we hope!

To make a long story short, we plan to be "down your way" next June and wondered if you wouldn't mind putting us up (and putting up with us, ha ha) for a little while? We're not a particularly big family – not by Irish standards anyway – and the nine of us could easily get by with a couple of rooms. I know you'd hate to think of us stuck in some old motel, and to be honest, there isn't a hope in hell we could manage that. The dole here – I think you call it welfare, is the pits, and if it wasn't for our Mary's parttime escort service and young Gary's private car parts operation we'd hardly be able to even raise the fare. But we're not going to desert Jack's Army now.

We don't plan to be with you much longer than three or four weeks – though we might stay on for a little break afterwards, as it would be a shame not to see something of your lovely country.

Looking forward to hearing from you,

Your loving nephew,

Joe.

Dear Auntie Lettie,

Thanks for your letter – and such a quick reply too.

We were all very sorry to hear about your leprosy infection and your present husband's regular outbreaks of beri-beri, Bright's Disease and yellow fever. Of course American medicine is the best in the world, so no doubt you'll both be back in the best of health before we arrive. God knows you'd want to be, as Chrissy says! Chrissy has a great sense of humour.

We were sorry also to hear how your house had been so badly affected by the fallout from the Malibu bushfires, the recent Venezuela hurricane, the eruption of Mount Hekla in Iceland, the defoliation problems in Katmandu, the tropical cooling problems in Malaysia, the Antarctic ice-cap temperature changes and the depletion in the ozone layer. You certainly have had your share of misfortunes. Still, I bet you're well insured. Remind me to tell you how *we* milk the insurance crowd over here: hit them for everything you can, that's my advice. Those bastards have more money than they know what to do with.

Anyway, I'm sure the house will be shipshape again by June, when you can be sure our visit will cheer you up. We might be a noisy family (especially little Mikey) but as any of our neighbours would tell you, we certainly know how to enjoy ourselves. Granny is already getting really excited, though we have to keep *that* under control, as she tends to have the odd little "plumbing problem" when we don't keep her calm.

Looking forward to hearing from you,

Your loving nephew,

Joe.

Dear Auntie Lettie,

Listen: our Willo can hardly wait to sort out those vicious neighbours of yours, and you can tell them from him he isn't in the least scared by their stock of weapons. In fact he's very impressed that you can buy an interballistic missile over the counter – America sounds like his kind of country, he says.

Now as for those plans for a twelve-lane highway cutting through your lovely home just days before our planned arrival, well, Chrissy is the one to fill you in on ways and means of dealing with planning officials. Her own record is something else. Corpo 1, Chrissy 67 is the score as we put it.

I'm sorry to hear you won't be there yourself when we arrive, because of your urgent business in Outer Mongolia. You won't forget the key under the mat? And the code to turn off that electric shock alarm system you mentioned? As for your three Rottweillers and the five pit bull terriers, young Micko's two bull mastiffs are looking forward to meeting them. Cheers!

Your loving nephew,

Joe.

P.S. I can understand how you feel, but how was I to know your husband was in the insurance racket?

JUST LOOKING FOR A LITTLE PUBLICITY

Apparently weary of publicity, Princess Diana announced a gradual withdrawal from public life...

I really shouldn't have to make this announcement myself, but have not yet had time to appoint a press team. The thing is, I have decided to leave private life. Not entirely of course. But at the end of this year, when I have completed my diary of private engagements, I shall be throwing myself fully into the public eye. I intend to scale down drastically my private duties, not least the ironing on Wednesday nights. All I want now is time, space and worldwide adulation.

When I began my private life all those years ago, I understood that the media would have no interest in it. But I was not aware of how overwhelming their lack of attention would prove to be. I have passed these wilderness years meeting dozens of people, none of them in the least well known, or ever likely to be. I have now had enough. I want to move among the beautiful people, where fame, glamour, exotic holidays and platinum Amex cards are taken for granted. I simply can't wait any longer.

I hope you will all forgive me, therefore, if I take this opportunity to share with you my plans for the future. I could not sit here today and make this sort of statement without acknowledging the complete lack of interest you, the public, have hitherto shown.

As you very well know, I have never been one for charities. However, all this will now change. Public life, as everyone knows, is a severe drain on the finances. So I will be putting my case to various charitable trusts, and I am relying on you to do the same.

I will also be open to any offers of posts, preferably the non-honorary variety, as patron, and if necessary matron. I intend to throw myself into these with vigour, just as soon as I verify the entertainment allowances and update my passport. I also plan to to help raise the profile of worthwhile and unjustly neglected causes, and have already been investigating sexual stereotyping in computer video games, the ludicrously low decibel levels permitted on sonic car alarms and the IFA's refusal to recognise the rights of slug-farmers.

I know you will all be with me in this. Already I have been inundated with a phone-call of support. From the bottom of my heart, I thank you all in advance.

Irish Times Commoner Correspondent Iggy Mullarkey, writes:

Hidden behind the smiling mask of a happy-go-lucky hack lay a deeply tormented soul. Starved of publicity, he lived a superficially glamorous life on a national newspaper but in reality suffered soul-destroying privacy. With the agony of complete obscurity becoming more painful all the time – there were many moments of dark despair – the deep-felt need to go public became more pressing. When he took his children to the park or the funfair, no one took pictures. Or if they did, they charged him a hefty price. *(heaps more of this stuff elsewhere in the paper).*

Lord Walter Witherington Crushby, commenting on the bombshell news, said: "We are very sorry to hear this, but clearly the aristocracy cannot be opened to every Tom, Dick and Harry – isn't that the phrase? The man's contribution to private life has probably been immense, though obviousy one can't be sure about this, and one understands his wish to leave behind all the ignominy it involves, but in the end of the day, what can one do? It isn't as if he's one relation, after all."

In order to help the media and *paparazzi*, I append my list of engagements for tomorrow.

9.30 am Breakfast in Mick's Caff, Lower Gardiner Street.

11.00 Work-out in Joe's Slimquik Gym, back of Phibsoro Bus Depot.

12.30 pm Working lunch, Coman's of Rathgar.

2.00 to 5.00 Informal recreation module, Mulligans of Poolbeg Street.

7.00 Official inauguration of Nonenties Unlimited.

7.15 Adjournment to The Long Hall, Sth Gt George's Street.

8.15 Pre-dinner shopping trip, McCabes, Mount Merrion.

9.00 Dinner: Starvin' Marvins, Westmoreland Street.

11.30 Informal Extravision visit, Lower Rathmines Road. (New Titles Section).

On other pages:

- *Why the cameras couldn't care less*
- *"Honey, I shrank the coverage" – a mother's tale*
- *Into the Limelight and editorial comment*

STRIKING THE WRONG NOTE ON THE PIANO

The Australian film, The Piano, was responsible for some discordant notes...

Around this time of year many families make a major and lifechanging decision: they buy a piano. It isn't always a good idea.

For those contemplating such a purchase, there is a film currently playing which will serve as a salutary lesson. It is called, with admirable directness, *The Piano*.

The film critics, though lavish in their praise, have entirely missed the point of *The Piano*. On the surface the film is indeed a steamy tale of brutal passion and repressed sexuality. But its real subject is the potential perils of piano possession, and its 1850s setting does not in the least detract from its relevance today.

The tale is simple enough. A Scottish widow, Ada, leaves home for colonial New Zealand and an arranged marriage to a man she has never met. With her she takes her piano and her daughter, in that order. The piano causes trouble, as you might expect.

From the outset, talented director Jane Campion provides subtly coded messages. Ada is a *widow*. The piano is there, the husband is gone. Doesn't that make you think? Moreover, Ada is a *Scottish* widow. And everyone knows that one of the prime sources of piano-purchase loans is the Scottish Widows and Orphans Fund. Why New Zealand? Clearly, because that's usually where people go if they are geographically disoriented, or wish to play the piano on their own. There is a lot of empty space in New Zealand, and it's just as well.

Ada never speaks at all. Quite deliberately, she remains mute. Straight away, the alert viewer guesses she is having trouble with whatever "easy-stages" piano rental-purchase scheme she has entered, and simply refuses to answer the phone or the door. Eventually she is forced to emigrate.

The critics make their first mistake when they write off Ada's new husband Stewart as a cold unfeeling man, too mean to transport Ada's piano across New Zealand. I wonder if those selfsame critics have ever tried to shift a piano from one side of a room to another (household pianos are by definition always on the wrong side of the room), never mind across a few thousand miles of impenetrable jungle and lumpy countryside? If not, they have no right to criticise Stewart.

Visual and aural connections are subtly created in the viewer's consciousness. What other famous and eccentric instrument-player was an elective mute? Yes: Harpo Marx, who played the harp, and whose brother Chico played the piano. This is Jane Campion's eloquent Marx Brothers *homage*: you've got to be that little bit crazy to own a piano, it's always a family problem, and there's no point in talking about it.

The exception proves the rule. Just think of our own John O'Conor: he plays the piano perfectly, loves talking, is quite sane, and (as proof of the latter) has never yet to my knowledge toured New Zealand. *Neither is he a widow.* Is it all coming together now?

Anyway, with a piano, a disturbed widow, a small child and a family-to-be, the movie stage is set for calamity, which duly arrives in the figure of Baines. Why is Baines so obviously dangerous? Because he rants on about Maori rights? No: because he is an adult male seeking piano lessons.

Such an individual is immediately dubious. In the old days, a woman wishing to qualify as a piano teacher had to weigh at least 15 stone, possess a violent temper and an inordinate dislike of small children. A criminal record helped too. In recent times the qualification requirements have been greatly relaxed, so that today's piano teacher is more likely to be an attractive young college graduate who actually likes her pupils, and can put them at ease when practising their *arpeggios*. Unfortunately this sometimes attracts the wrong kind of pupil, a fact Ada finds out to her cost. Suffice to say that while we've all done barter deals in our day, Baines's ideas on the matter are just outrageous.

In the second half of the movie the three adults have to face the consequences of their actions. This happens to everyone who lets a piano into the house. Be warned.

THE BIRTH OF POETRY, THE POETRY OF BIRTH

I was delighted to note the imaginative appointment of eminent poet Eavan Boland to the post of writer-in-residence at the National Maternity Hospital. This is certainly a change from the way they do things in the UK, where writers-in-residence appear to reside mainly in prisons: Brixton, Gartree, Franklands and Wakefield so far.

But there are, as Ms Boland has pointed out in this newspaper, certain challenges involved. With no clear structure outlined for her, she plans to proceed on a "trial and error" basis (perhaps it's just as well her appointment was not to Mountjoy) and she speaks of "a continuous process of collaboration to see what works". One might be forgiven for concluding she has not the remotest idea of what the job may entail.

Fortunately, I myself can offer what I hope is useful advice, based on my stint back in the Sixties as poet-in-residence at a State maternity hospital which for professional reasons (theirs and mine) I had better not name.

I was in my early twenties in those days, and had had a small *success d'estime* with each of my two slim collections, *Stunned and Deliver* and *Foetal Attraction*. (The possibility that the hospital administrators had read no further than these titles did not upset me in the least).

I began my first morning round in St Agatha's, a pre-natal ward with about thirty women. Rather than have myself formally introduced by Matron, I simply walked to the middle of the room and began to declaim from my well-known threnody, *Pulse of the Premature Chaffinch.*

At the outset, there was not a sound to be heard but the chattering of 30 women about to share a universal experience. And when I had ceased reading, I realised the chattering had not stopped even for a single moment. *I had gone completely unnoticed.*

The poetic rightness of this made me almost swoon. To think that a poet, and a male poet at that, could be so fully subsumed into this life-filled, life-giving community of mothers-to-be. The purity and unity of their non-response touched me more than I can say.

The spell was suddenly broken by loud screams from Dolores, who was expecting twins – and whose dual expectations were realised there and then about three minutes later. Can you imagine what witnessing such a scene meant to a poet like myself? I am certain I should have written something remarkable on the spot had I not simply fainted.

I was brought around to hoots of laughter from these jolly women, and bawdy jokes about morning sickness and the like. I can't tell you what this warm, near-animalistic response meant to my poetic soul.

Anyway they sat me up in bed, plumped up my pillows and fed me kiwi squash and pink marshmallows and unseeded raisins and chocolate eggs and Mikado biscuits and banana ice-cream sundaes and Sugar Frosties and kumquats – all the magical little treats with which women in this state (pregnancy, I mean, not Ireland) are wont to indulge themselves. I can say now that the germs of perhaps my finest lyric poem, *Craving Lunatics*, lay in this very experience.

But my greatest triumphs were outside the delivery rooms, where I had the perfect audience – men who were haggard, worried, sleepless, sullen, apprehensive and resigned. (I must admitted I later toyed with the title *Corridors of Powerless*). And it was from their ranks, one busy morning, came the young man who begged me to take his place by his wife's side as she gave birth. He "couldn't stand" the prospect himself, he confided in blunt English. And the surgical mask would hide my face. As a creative artist, open to all human experience, how could I resist?

When the time came, all went well for a while. My "wife" held firm to my hand while I mopped her brow, all the time filtering the experience through the prism of my poetic imagination. Just as the baby arrived, however, my mask slipped (literally, I mean) and seeing me, the poor woman screamed in horror. I began to launch into an explanation of the role of the poet as a kind of midwife, but the nurse, misunderstanding, bundled me out. "Don't worry," she reassured me, "rejection isn't unusual in this game."

To this day I do not know if she was speaking of the new mother and her baby, or of my profession; but as a poet, of course, such ambiguities are my stock in trade.

SOCIETY LIFE CAN POSE ITS PROBLEMS

I was reading in this newspaper recently about the lady who has established the brand-new Irish Byron Society. Clearly an inveterate setter-up of societies, Ms Mary Caulfield is also a co-founder of the Irish Haiku Society but is "fed up" trying to compose the things and now hopes to set up a limerick society instead.

I have an idea of how she feels. Establishing a literary group of any sort, helping to guide it and maintaining one's own enthusiasm is by no means easy. I ought to know.

Many years ago, I was a founder member of the very first Irish Haiku Society. The initial interest was substantial enough; it was when we held our inaugural meeting that the trouble started.

I had noticed in our gathering an unusual number of young and rather muscular young men, and indeed was delighted that a haiku group should attract such youthful interest, even if it did contrast rather strikingly with our mostly middle-aged members.

At the outset I thought it appropriate to explain the nature of haiku, though – just as one would expect an ornithology club to know something of birds – I presumed most of those present already knew a little about the classical Japanese poem format.

I really shouldn't have had to stress the obvious, but in retrospect it was perhaps just as well. Straight away the group of young men, all of them dressed in black leather, stood up in disgust and walked out.

No doubt young people who so often jump to conclusions without thinking are prone to this sort of error, but really, the martial arts are quite well defined in their own way and I find it very hard to understand how any educated person could confuse them with age-old verse forms.

Perhaps I should not have resorted to sarcasm by pointing out that there are no black belts awarded in haiku, but surely there was no need for these young men to respond with an aggressive scissor-kicking demonstration, which caused a good deal of nervous upset among our older members.

After this initial discord, things went reasonably well for a while, until our haiku group ran into the same problem Ms Caulfield has encountered: they got fed up trying to compose the things. My own opinion is that, even in those days, discipline was waning. One participant insisted on regularly sneaking in an extra line, others saw no "point" in the syllable restrictions, and so on. I was disappointed, though hardly surprised, when many of our little group seceded to our foolishly liberal and verbose competitor, the Free Verse Society.

So we eventually disbanded, and like Ms Caulfield, by sheer coincidence, I turned my attention to the establishment of this country's first limerick society.

You can guess of course the initial misunderstanding that arose. What is it about Shannonsiders that should make them imagine people would want to celebrate their particular county? I need hardly add that not one of the Limerick enthusiasts was a limerick enthusiast.

But the principal problem with a limerick society is the kind of people it inevitably attracts. Their interests are usually what you might call elemental, and I also came across individuals who, sadly, appeared to have less interest in the prosody than the "punchline".

There were more worrying problems. One night we were reciting, for purely stimulatory purposes, the rightly-renowned limerick about the "young man of St John's". Word got out, however, and to our horror we subsequently found ourselves accused of slander and embroiled in litigation with the St. John's dons' descendants and the trustees of the college. It was when we were also sued by something called the "Swan Protection Committee" that I was finally forced to wind up our little group.

Some years later I made desultory attempts to establish a sonnet society, only to see it split most acrimoniously into three bitterly opposed factions – Petrarchan, Miltonian and Shakespearean – each ludicrously asserting the superior nature of its own format. After that I more or less retired, but did come back to found, join – and run singlehandedly – a somewhat unusual group: my Solitaire Society *is* rather exclusive but on the whole I find it less stressful.

SHELVING THE ISSUE IN THE DIY HOME

"There is nothing difficult about putting up a shelf. Yet numerous DIY surveys show it is the job most often deferred."

I came across these remarks recently in a piece by a handyman-writer who went on to give some "practical" advice on the whole business of shelving.

Not everybody will be aware, of course, that shelving has very little to do with practicality, and much more to do with fear, guilt, shame and humiliation. I should know. I once worked on the most famous of all DIY surveys, the 1957 Haart-Baumfeld Inquiry, whose initiators became renowned as "the Masters and Johnson of the DIY world."

The findings on shelf construction were so shocking that they were kept hidden from the public for many years.

When the project began, I was a junior door-to-door researcher. Superficially, my brief was straightforward: I was to ask householders about the details of their DIY projects. In reality, I was to secretly investigate the success (or, and usually, otherwise) of their shelving projects.

It was easy enough for an experienced eye like mine to pick out DIY enthusiasts in any area. A "rockery" looking more like a lunar excavation was a dead giveaway. A front garden bird-house leaning at an angle of more than 20° was another good sign. A boot-scraper made from compressed tin cans confirmed suspicions straightaway.

Having picked the right house, there was rarely any problem in being allowed in. "Jack!" the wife might cry out (I could never get over how often the husband's name was Jack) "someone doing a DIY survey!"

Jack would emerge from a cloud of dust and a background noise of drilling, chain-sawing and anglegrinding, and greet me as if I were bringing news of a Lottery win. When the dust cleared, there he would stand, a vision of ecstatically fulfilled Do-It-Yourself manhood. His only problem would be what to show me first.

Would it be the shower he had "rigged up" (why do DIY people never use words like "installed"?) in the guest bedroom? Would it be the guest bedroom itself, the one he created by "knocking together" (that awful pseudo-deprecatory language again) an unused cutlery drawer and half the dog's kennel? Would it be his attic perversion, excuse, me, conversion, which anyone could now use as a "play area"? Anyone, that is, not higher than 30 inches, able to see in the dark, laugh at skin grazes and exist without oxygen.

Inexorably, I would lead the conversation towards the dreaded topic of shelving. Jack would feebly try to change the subject, but as we used to say in our business, "poor assemblers make poor dissemblers". Before long, all the pathetic evidence would be laid bare.

Even now, years later, I remember those subdued evenings with my colleagues in the Haart-Baumfeld offices, annotating and differentiating the various shelf disasters for our professional purposes. Someone like poor Jack might have known them all. There were the "saggers" with their give-away median droop; the "hammocks", saggers in their death throes; the "sliders", their books huddled together like over-ambitious skiers crashed at the bottom of a steep slope; the "tippers", which hadn't taken account of a bulging back wall; the "zigzaggers" on their confusing trail in a hopelessly off-plumb alcove; the "swallowers" yawning backwards into the void; and the ubiquitous "lookers" – fine until something of substance, e.g. a fly, landed and brought them crashing down.

A typical Jack might bluster or try to laugh off his doomed shelving efforts. But inevitably he would collapse in tears. His wife would join us and we would all have a warming little chat about material choice, plumb-lines, support structures, templates and counter-sinking. Then Jack would dry his tears, have a cup of tea and, enthusiasm rising again, lead me off to see how he "dealt" (more or less, and more often the latter) with the rising damp, or how he re-roofed the house for $9\frac{1}{2}$ pence with a cunning combination of rattan cane, wallpaper paste and thumb-tacks.

We learned a lot about shelving but, as you can imagine, even more about people.

WOMEN OPT FOR A MORE ACTIVE LUNCH LIFE

I see from a survey in *Good Housekeeping* magazine (the answer is yes, and why shouldn't I?) that a great many women prefer being wined and dined in restaurants to making love.

The way this was worded, I thought at first it meant these women preferred wining and dining in restaurants to making love in restaurants, but it seems not. The latter preference, if it exists at all (I have an awful feeling it does), was not mentioned.

Many men, particularly the married species, may well react badly to news of this survey, and wonder why a couple of hours spent in an unfamiliar dining-room, often packed with complete strangers, should prove so attractive. But more thoughtful men will see the findings for what they are: a clear reflection of rising restaurant standards.

After all, women's avowed preference for lunch to sex is hardly surprising when one thinks of the really excellent choice on most restaurant lunch menus these days, the general ease of booking, the widespread acceptance of credit cards, the novelty factor of different dining partners, and the fact that it isn't rude to tell your companion you have to be back in the office by 2.30 pm.

But I have been thinking long (and hard) about the more important implications. If the subscribers to *Good Housekeeping* are so keen on being taken out to lunch, surely the housekeeping suffers? And the more difficult question has to be asked: what has sex to do with housekeeping at all?

In an effort to find answers, I talked to a number of good housekeepers, regular purchasers of the magazine whose name implies devotion to their interests.

Marian was typical. She buys *Good Housekeeping* every month and spends perhaps an hour and a half reading it. "Though of course I would never even open it until I had the beds made and the ironing done and the evening meal prepared."

And what would her favourite articles be?

Marian: "Well, I always take advantage of the special offers and I am regularly on the lookout for useful tips on dust-removing. Kitchen-sink scourers are another major passion of mine, but I am disappointed to say that in the last five years, I have not yet seen a single feature on this particular subject, though there seems to be unlimited space for articles like *Orgies and the Over-80s – Why the Fuss?* and *Accepting Your Lover's Mackerel Fetish*, to name but two."

And what of the magazine's famed dinner party recipes? "Oh, I never forget to cut them out every month."

"So at least you get good value from this section of the magazine? You use the recipes?"

"Well, not exactly. But I keep them in perfect condition in the adorable ring file I got on special offer from the magazine."

It was a joy to listen to a sensible subscriber like Marian, if a little tiring after three hours. But how did she feel about the survey on sex versus lunch?

Marian was astonished and horrified. She hadn't even noticed it.

As my investigation proceeded, I discovered that a magazine's readers are not always what one might expect. The thought even occurred to me that *Good Housekeeping* might not be for good housekeepers at all, but merely for people who *possess*, or perhaps just like to possess, good housekeepers. And on feeding all my information into the computer, I discovered that for every subscriber with a genuine interest in good housekeeping, there were 2.3 individuals who by some odd coincidence always turned straight to the more gratuitous material, and indeed read little else.

When I returned to Marian with these findings, she was cynical enough to remark that it was probably the 2.3 factor who filled in the sex/lunch survey.

Anyway, with the help of her Tuesday-morning "Dust-Busters" group, Marian is now organising a lobby to Keep Magazine Contents in Touch with Their Titles. But I fear she will not get very far. She is thinking along the lines of a survey, and I doubt that any magazine will touch it. They have their readers to think about, after all.

DOWN AND OUT WITH GER IN ESSEX

I see where Germaine Greer, the feminist and academic, is to sue a *Mail on Sunday* journalist who posed as a down-and-out and was received into her Essex home after newspaper reports suggested she was opening her home to the destitute. Ms Greer had earlier asserted that hospitality is "a sacred duty" of all privileged people and explained her empathy for the homeless: "I have slept on pillows that smelt of other people's saliva, lived with sofas that stank of other people's incontinence and cigarettes, endured communal bathrooms smeared with every kind of body product." One is tempted to ask – why? But let it pass.

As it happens, I myself was for a period in the Seventies among the destitute, and after a depressing few weeks in London I decided to try my luck in the county of Essex. One cold January evening, I found myself, hungry, thirsty and tired – or "HTT" as we tramps ironically knew it – just outside the lovely village of Saffron Walden.

Having by this time learnt that I was just as likely to get some help from those of modest means as from the rich, I approached a rather shabby-looking house. When the door was opened I was greeted in silence by a woman who stood at least six foot six in her (stockinged) feet. "Ger!" shouted this impressive vision – "come quick!" I recoiled, expecting to see some angry man come and dismiss me; instead I found myself greeted by a doe-eyed middle-aged lady.

Now as a tramp I had often been stared at, but Ger and Shell (as her companion was named) gaped as if at a Martian. They took in my threadbare jacket, my newspaper socks, my old bedroll. For some odd reason, they seemed to be absolutely delighted with me.

"Are you homeless?" asked Shell breathlessly. I didn't have time to answer as she went on. "Hungry? Thirsty? Are you absolutely and utterly destitute?"

I nodded. It was all I could do.

They looked at each other in unrestrained joy. They hugged me. They kissed me.

To my utter shame, they smelt me. And then they manhandled me into their kitchen.

Shell hurried off to "rustle up" some dinner, while Ger sat across from me, her huge eyes and wispy grey hair only inches from my face.

I was beginning to worry about where all this was leading and felt it was time to explain my simple needs. "If I could just have a sandwich and maybe a glass –"

Ger raised her magnificent chin. "I am you," she announced passionately.

I looked around, but there was no one else present.

"I am one with you," Ger went on. "I have slept on pillows that smelt of other people's saliva, lived with sofas that stank of other people's incontinence and cigarettes, endured communal bathrooms smeared with every kind of body product."

Responding to this sort of remark is never easy, but I did my best. "I'm off the cigarettes for the last 10 days," I told her.

Ger appeared not to hear me. "Hospitality," she went on, stroking my filthy sleeve, "is a sacred duty of all privileged people."

I was beginning to look surreptitiously around for possible exits when Shell came in with the dinner. It wasn't bad, for steamed grass, and while I ate, Ger read from her favourite author, Ginny Woolf, I think she said, and from some Big House tale, *Ratcliff Hall*, if memory does not deceive. Shell then sluiced out our earthenware dinner-bowls, banked up the fire with dried cowpats and began to chop logs in the living room with a long-handled axe, all the while loudly singing *If I Were a Rich Man* in a distinctly ribald version of her own.

For all I know, this might well have been considered a homely evening scene in Saffron Walden in the seventies, but to say I was nervous would be a clear understatement.

In the end I just had to make a run for it. Even now, 20 years on, I have nightmares. "Wait!" I can still hear Ger shrieking. "I've slept on pillows that smelt of other people's saliva! I've lived with sofas. . ."

It's possible I may one day go back to Saffron Walden and recommend Ger and Shell a nice hostel packed with destitutes for them to visit. But now that I've joined the ranks of the privileged I just don't know if I would be all that welcome.

CYN AND THE SECRETS OF GIRL TALK

I see where Cynthia Ní Mhurchú, newly-appointed co-presenter (with Gerry Ryan) of the Eurovision Song Contest, has been outlining her views to a reporter on the subject of men, women and conversation – or as the paper put it more seductively, the "secrets of girl talk".

Cynthia believes that men and women have a different approach to communication. "Men like to talk about the here and now. Women like to tease things out. The men will say 'Oh the women are going deep again'. Women talk less about headline stuff and soccer results and more about themselves in the world."

There were more fascinating insights like this, with Cynthia sounding a cautious note to the effect that since women were now more "involved in everything" and in general "more part of the action", there was a "knock-on" effect on men. "It's not a great advantage to have men doubt themselves. I like to see a balance where one is not dominating the other."

Oddly enough, shortly after reading this I found myself (careless to have lost myself in the first place, I know) accidentally overhearing two vaguely familiar voices. But herewith the chat as it occurred.

Cyn: I was just thinking, Ger, about my rise to fame, I mean of course our rise, the fact that I –

Ger: I –

Cyn: I just think it's important that we speak out on the big night with wit and warmth and *savoir faire* and *laissez faire* and any other *faire* we can get to grips with, and your French isn't really all that good is it Ger? So it seems to me that I –

Ger: I –

Cyn: – should perhaps present, so to speak, rather a good deal of the Song Contest, now of course I'm not saying the whole thing, not at all, but perhaps considering that after all the audience, let's face it, will expect lots of female glamour and a really big smile, and of course –

Ger: I –

Cyn: It isn't that I'm saying you haven't got all of my qualities, well, bar the legs ha ha! joke, Ger, and the flowing blonde hair, it's just that what I'm thinking of here is what the audience wants, and frankly, no offence at all of course Ger but while your TV show is wonderful in its own way and no bigger fan as you know than my little self I just wonder if it isn't just that teeny teeny bit you know, well, *vulgar,* honestly but did you want to say something?

Ger: I –

Cyn: Because if you did you know that in this job being a good listener is perhaps the most important thing of all and I know men and women are different you like to talk about the here and now –

Ger: I –

Cyn: – and what matters in the here and now is just how much hype and fame I, I mean we, can get out of this thing and we women you see like to tease things out. And personally I have no time at all for people who say Eurovision is *just* a song contest, I mean really, that *just* annoys me I hate being patronised and I'm sure you have very interesting views on that Ger as you do on everything.

Ger: I –

Cyn: What I was going to say was that I think your views, a man's views, are very important too and you aren't all just into headline news and who beat Poland and those poor peasants in Bosnia you know I was on a gorgeous hol to Poric once it's on the east coast or is it the west anyway it was really super, to think a holiday destination should disappear from the brochures like that it's just tragic someone has a lot to answer for and of course some men can express their feminine side, though not too much I always say God knows there's enough of that where *we* work after all and see themselves in the real world where they can discuss the Eurovision Song Contest in a way that reflects something positive and attractive, Ger –

Ger: I –

Cyn: Which is why, Ger, I really want to ask your advice Ger so let's stop all this foolish talk about *me* and let me ask you now Ger what do *you* really really think of my left profile?

Ger: I –

Cyn: You're right. It *is* my best side. Isn't –

Ger: I –

Cyn: Oh Ger – you're not of those men who insist on having the last word, are you?

COME BACK, PADDY REILLY, ALL IS FORGIVEN

Paddy Reilly, the hero of Percy French's famous song, was a real-life person in the 19th century who left Cavan to go abroad.

I have nothing at all against Torvill and Dean, but I do think this "comeback" phenomenon whereby former stars of stage, screen, politics, sport and sew on (those unsung heroes of the needlework world) try to repeat former triumphs, is getting out of hand. (When was it ever in hand, you might well ask).

You never spoke truer word.

Oh. And you are – ?

Paddy Reilly.

Not of Ballyjamesduff?

The same.

May I say how pleased I am to welcome you back after all your years away.

I'm not back. I'm only here on a visit. Incognito, so keep it quiet.

Mr Reilly. Have you any idea how many tenors in lounge bars and at wedding receptions all over the country have been plaintively begging you over many years to return to your native village?

I have a very good idea. Manny's the time I heard them meself, and devil the one I ever heard with a note in his head.

So are you now responding to their pleas? Are you in fact planning a comeback?

I'm thinking about it. I won't deny that.

But aren't you concerned at what happened to Torvill and Dean, John McEnroe, George Foreman –

Torvill O'Dean was done out of it, by rights he should have got the gold medal. The way he kept out of your one's way, never bumped into her even the wance, was magic. I never saw dancing like that in all me life, and that ice is slippier than anny dance hall floor, I was told that by someone who knows. Very aisy to take a tumble, smash your hip bone to smithereens and lave your legs in bloody ribbons. The balance is everything.

Mr Reilly, now that you are here in the flesh, there are various matters that one would like to clear up.

Oh fire away.

Why did you leave Ballyjamesduff in the first place?

None of your business.

I must put it to you that there are certain rumours in circulation. Specifically, that you are in fact, "old" Reilly, of Reilly's Daughter infamy. That you are her father. Further, that you played on the big bass drum, had a mind for murder and slaughter, and a single bright red glittering eye (which you kept on your lovely daughter). Do you deny this?

That's all damn lies. Can't ye see I have two good eyes still? But Big Martin O'Reilly was a first cousin of mine once removed, and a dangerous man to cross. There was bad blood there. It goes back a long way.

Would you care to elaborate?

Giddy I-ae, Giddy-I-ae (bang bang bang), play it on your old bass drum.

I should also point out that you are wanted on charges of assault.

What?

It is well documented that you "took long Magee by the scruff, for slanderin' Rosie Kilrain, then marchin' him straight out of Ballyjamesduff, assisted him into a drain."

Those Magees were all the same, he deserved no better nor what he got. That's all I have to say about that. "Oh sweet are the dreams as the dudeen I puff, of whisperin' over the sea – "

I want to ask now about your apparent promiscuity and racist attitudes.

What?

I have written evidence in your own hand that you "loved the young women of every land, that always came easy to me, just barrin' the belles of the blackamoor brand and the chocolate shapes of Feegee."

I reject that entirely! I have nothing against the blacks, the bestlooking woman I ever saw was the colour of coal. And if I planted me wild oats, I only did what came natural, but Rosie Kilrain was the only girl I ever loved. I don't suppose she waited for me be any chance?

She has, as they say, buried two husbands.

I'm sorry to hear that. Has she children?

Five, I believe, some of them with good jobs in the Civil Service. And I am told Rosie herself currently has an understanding with the local sergeant in Cootehill. Now a few more questions.

Not now, I'm on me way.

Come back, Paddy Reilly –

(*Later*: we turn left on the bridge at Finea, stop halfway to Cootehill, meet Rosie Kilrain, her family and friends, and learn more of Paddy Reilly's background).

104

DE MORTUIS NIL NISI BUNKUM

As newspaper reading experiences go, the only thing to beat a really good obituary is a really bad obituary. I mean one which puts the boot in while twisting the knife in a still-warm back (and damned difficult it is to keep a newish corpse propped on its side, too). Unfortunately, even among journalists, so-called good manners and a sense of misplaced decency usually keep these simple reading joys to a minimum.

I keep an eye on the obituary-writers. Never know when I might need one. No! No! Please nurse, you don't understand! Thormley-Greer of *The Times* is the only man for this job! Yes I know I'm only on Plan B but I thought – who? WHO? *Phil Crumpley?* Of the *Sun?* For God's sake, nurse!

Obituarists are, of course, notorious for the use of cliché. I am not concerned here with the ordinary but perfectly respectable obituary clichés which have stood the test of time, how he/she triumphed over failure, had more to him/ her than met the eye, and whose upbringing and virtues and unfailing good nature stood him/her in good stead. I have no argument with these. (Man arrested for provoking row with cliché in public place: Hey head! Yeah, you, *Triumph-over-Failure*, who are ye lookin' at?).

But there is other stuff.

He/she was a success for all the wrong reasons. Opportunity to list unappetising characteristics of deceased.

Was his/her own worst enemy. As above, but sets up for more personal attack.

The irresistible force of his/her beauty/wit/knowledge/charm met the immovable object of his/her personality/character/honesty. Handy Polyfilla cliché, fills crack/space until reader moves on.

He/she recognised his/her own faults. Which I now list.

If he/she showed occasional lapses of judgement. Which I now list.

In a lighter vein, he/she etc. What? You didn't realise that the obituarist has been dealing with blood-carrying vessels of weight unspecified but *heavier* than those now to be considered?

He/she was, in short. I realise I have gone on a bit.

There is fancier stuff. When Melina Mercouri died recently, one fellow described her as "the poor man's Anna Magnani, the rich man's Lila Kedrova." That put a lot of readers in their (ignorant) place, you can bet. There was more where that came from – listen to this: "*In their first collaboration, Celui qui doit morir – an intolerably pretentious version of Kazantzaki's Christ Recrucified –*" Oh, right.

And in their ninth collaboration, *Tempus Fugit, And Well He Might* – an ineffably tedious rap rendering of Aristophanes' *The Frogs*.

He/she was the quintessence of. Goodness, professionalism, charm, etc. Quintessence. Ah yes. Wonderful ontropranoorial success in the production of Quinn T'Essence, the devastating Celto-Gallic cologne wowing the international perfume world from the Rue Chatelaine to Rio, available in spray-on, roll-on and atomizer, 50mls, 100mls, right up to and including five-gallon drums. Quinn T'Essence, the fragrance for today.

His/her name has become synonymous with. Right. I have to nail this one down so it won't get up again in a hurry. Say the pithecoid bone-lazy meths-shattered obituarist turning out this stuff avers that the name of the lately-deceased viola player (sidesaddle version) Wilhelmina Zuckwart, about whom he is "writing", is "snyomymous" with style. So next morning you are going down the street, and who passes you by (with a wink of her bright blue eye, God help us, that lumpeen of glass is better than a gaping hole but a good jocular surgeon, only joking, I mean ocular, could have saved the other one if he got there in time) but the very smart-looking Máirín Beag O'Shaughnessy. And you remark innocently to your pal: "Oh, that girl has wonderful Wilhelmina Zuckwart." Your companion is totally bemused and it takes you an hour to explain your meaning. You then know to your cost that Ms Zuckwart's name, whatever else it might be, is *not* synonymous with style. So that obituarist is a fool or a liar.

Oops, it's the Corrs and Clars Col Again

I see where the American figure skater Nancy Kerrigan has been rebuilding her image of late, after putting her foot in things earlier on. During a Disney parade in Florida, shortly after she returned from the Winter Olympics in Norway, Miss Kerrigan was overheard remarking, "This is the corniest thing I've ever done. But when recently hosting the Saturday Night Live show, she explained that what she *meant* to say was that posing with Mickey Mouse was "the *horniest* thing" she had ever done.

Good girl Nancy, lots of you "liberals" might be thinking. Well, you have the wrong end of the stick. The girl went up a lot in my estimation when she expressed her scorn for Mickey Mouse. But as far as I'm concerned she's gone right down again with that class of back-sliding, not to mention smutty language far from acceptable on a family show.

Don't get me wrong. Nancy Kerrigan on the whole seems a grand young woman, though personally I like a girl with maybe a bit more meat on her, a girl with spirit, individuality, a clear complexion, some knowledge of what goes on in the world, who leaves a clear plate after her at dinnertime, dresses warmly and sensibly in a way befitting the fairer sex, has a measure of ordinary common sense, a feeling of self-worth, hair kept well out of the eyes, decent morals, sound family background (study the mother carefully is good advice) and a well-rounded personality.

You're not averse to a well-rounded bosom either is what I hear.

Do you always have to be bringing in that class of chat? The thing is, anyone can get things wrong. But the newspaper game is particularly dangerous. Say somebody like myself in the course of my "duties" makes a harmless mistake, accidentally insults some obscure poltroon, suggests he is a secret serial murderer or bigamist twice over, or ate his mother's gangrenous leg in order to stay alive after the plane crash on the Bangor Erris bog in 1934. Or whatever, some innocent remark, mild confusion, mistake anyone could make, happenabishop sort of thing, no offence intended.

What happens? The "injured party", a mean old social misfit egged on by his bitter widowed mother, out only for money and vengeance, takes offence. Employs his solicitor to send letters on fancy note-paper threatening all sorts of things up to and including closure of the newspaper and execution by garrotting of all its employees. The usual kind of oul' legal guff, not to be taken seriously. But the craven lot in charge of this paper backs down, denies me my moment of glory in court, and the result is I have to make a public apology which sticks in my craw and has to be dragged out of me word by word.

So I suppose I better get this over with. When I wrote recently that "The entertainer Joe Bogginsbottom was 49 last week, and there is still no sign of him growing up", what I actually meant of course was that there was still no sign of him *slowing* up. Similarly, when I said his art was a "useless reminder" of times gone by, what I naturally meant was a *useful* reminder.

I am pleased to give this apology as much prominence as the initial remarks and by way of compensation I have donated an agreed sum to a charity nominated by Mr. Bogginsbottom. I accept that I defamed him, that he is and always has been an upstanding performer of the highest artistic quality, held in high esteem by his peers.

There you are Bogginsbottom, you vicious old so-and-so. Now clear off. Don't ever expect to see your name mentioned here again. Not one more word of publicity will you ever receive in this newspaper as long as I have anything to do with it.

You and all belonging to you are finished. And I have *contacts*, people who matter. If you find your calls are not being returned, you'll know why. And in 10 or 20 years' time, when you're *weeping* for work on the chicken 'n' chips circuit, when your "successes" at the Braemor Rooms and the Old Shieling are long forgotten, when your drink problem has your children's children changing their names by deed poll, when your friends have long crossed to the other side of the street – you will have time to think.

What'll you have then but your ould single-column "equal prominence" apology, yellowed and dog-eared, and maybe the memory of the 50 quid which I very much doubt you ever handed over to the St. Vincent de Paul? You'll be sorry then when it's too late.

COMPLETE BALDERDASH SYNDROME BY PROXY

I read in *The Star*, whose medical coverage must be starting to worry them at *The Lancet*, about a brand-new brain disorder syndrome uncovered by London specialists "baffled" by a man who couldn't read a clock face. This poor fellow, a stroke victim, could read numbers and set the clock hands correctly – but couldn't read back what it showed. When asked the time he would give "very silly answers", though of course to a brain surgeon, I suppose answers to just about everything must be sorely disappointing.

The specialists have named the syndrome "horologagnosia". Sure what else would they call it.

The Star, and no doubt its readers, had a good chortle over this syndrome being a perfect excuse for tardiness in the workplace. Let them have their laff: we are a more serious newspaper and our crack unit of craniobrainio corrrespondents will take an indepth look at the logical, ontolgical, arceochrontolgical, jellioiocustardo-physiognomical, erantephshyiolestrycho-supra-nomi-caoli-garchical and ortroclaustral aspects.

Don't worry. We realise that few of our readers will be able to "keep up" with this discussion, so it will be a private consultation among our specialists over steaming pots of coffee ferried in – Stena Sealink the kind sponsors – from Bewley's , mounds of newlymade sandwiches from the same, and perhaps – we are not all the killjoys some make us out to be in the consultant correspondent world – a few bottles of stout from Doyle's. Then we shall unveil (Who's responsible for this? There was no need whatsoever to use that good Chinese brocade for the job) our findings in layman's terms. You have that to look forward to.

But syndrome nomenclature is truly one of the most fascinating areas of modern medicine. I saw a while back where a young American nanny, who got annoyed with the baby in her charge and therefore killed it, was defended by a sickiatrist (sick) who told the court the poor girl was suffering from "Adult Attention Deficiency Syndrome"

Doctor, doctor, nobody takes any notice of me!

Right, next please.

Okay. Not very funny. Not at all funny. Anthin' better to offer in the way of a joke? No? All right, here's wan that'll have you in stitches. Stop me if: Woman in surgery: "Doctor, I'm sufferin' somethin' terrible from the piles."

Doctor: "Right, my good woman, where are you bleeding from?"

Woman: "Finglas."

Hold it right there. Your Honour. I submit this male-female dialogue inter-change to be of fantastical origin and totally unacceptable. I call on the jury to find the defendant guilty of perpetrating heinously offensive socio-cultur-al crime under guise of Jocose Conversational Gambit, otherwise known as "joke". Offensive on a number of fronts, herein listed. Patronising male/female relationship ethos. Phrase "My good woman" indicative of Very Very Severe Occupational Condescenscion Sydnrome. Also, clear and incontrovertible evidence of Assumed Linguistic Deficiency Syndrome, whereby medical figure speech patterns are unfairly contrasted as being "superior" to unnamed woman in surgery, also unfairly deprived of title such as doctor, thus again victimising female victim. Perpetrator of joke also guilty . . .

Shut up a minute. I call on *my* defence, top sickiatrist Thompson Burnett Ph.D, M.Appl.Pysch (Sasketchwan), D. Phil (Nebraska Good Feelings Inst.). Go on Thomps, tell'em.

M'Lud: the defendant is an innocent victim of Class/Career Assumption Syndrome, whereby he foolishly assumes on current evidence medical spe-cialist unlikely to emerge from specific north Dublin background in ques-tion, hence his Unflattering Location Selection Syndrome. Also, my client is quite clearly suffering from Accent Embellishment Syndrome by Proxy, wherein he ascribes or projects presumed modes of speech outside himself—

I think we have all had enough of this.

WEEDS ARE JUST UNDERPRIVILEGED FLOWERS

I was deeply moved to hear of Mike Murphy defending the rights of the daffodil at the recent launch of Daffodil Day. Tears in his eyes, Mike told of how, after months in the cold earth, the daffs stick their heads above ground and begin to brighten the spring day with their happy yellow colour. And the next thing is, some woman cuts off their pretty heads and sticks them in a bunch with other daffs, total strangers whose sexuality is quite unknown and downright dubious.

Mike didn't say it, but we might as well reveal now that he is being stalked (sorry) as patron of our new Flower Power movement. This is no Sixties revivalist nonesense. No. It is all about taking a stand for the rights of flowers, their essential...flowerness, about taking them seriously. It is a call to arms, well, to roses, daffs, Sweet Williams, gardenias, dahlias – and, yes – weeds. We are nothing if not all-embracing.

I was fortunate enough to be granted an exclusive interiew with the secretary of the new movement, Petunia Mulch, who took me out to her garden, which she runs as a home from home for orphaned and abandoned flowers, and weeds.

In polite gardening language, you would describe Petunia's place as a riot of colour. Impolitely, it is simply a riot. Its mistress, however, prefers to call it an "untamed wilderness", though to look at Petunia you would not immediately cast her in the Indiana Jones mould. Nevertheless, she opened my eyes.

"Think," she asked me in her sad tinkly voice "of what is done in this crazed botanical world. The cuttings business; surgery without anaesthetic. The forced growth. The dismissal and death of unsatisfactory 'specimens'. The killing, colonising, theft, crossbreeding, elitism."

A whole pantheon of gardening criminals was evoked by Petunia. I began to think of the superficially normal gardeners I knew. Certain things began to fall into place.

It is embarrassing for me to report here that Petunia's "chief enemies" included the *Irish Times* writer/gardener Jim Reynolds. She drew my attention to a recent "unprovoked attack" of his; how he had announed that "it is never too late to start weeding". His advice about being "on the alert". About getting "the offenders" out while they are "small and manageable" ("read defenceless" said Petunia, pathetically). His warning about "troubles ahead".

Petunia was almost in tears at Jim's attack on what she called "poor defenceless weeds". Weeds were simply underprivileged flowers, she told me. They came from deprived backgrounds – from inner cities, where they had no education, no opportunities. Was it any wonder they turned to crime, infiltrating and feeding off the most select areas?

Petunia trembled. She took me along to where she was integrating some puny and illformed specimens of weed with roses and dahlias. All seemed to be fine, though I thought one or two of the roses had a somewhat disdainful look. Petunia noticed this too and gave them a good talking to; they had the grace to wilt.

"Gardeners don't even try to hide their cruelty," whispered Petunia as we walked on. She reminded me of how, on the Great British Garden Show on BBC recently, presenter Ruth Langsford candidly stated that "the best gardener is a mixture of tender nursemaid and ruthless murderer".

"I don't want it to look like I have something against the *Irish Times*", Petunia went on quietly, "but did you notice how your Mr Reynolds recently described the savage reality of weeding?"

Petunia pulled out a newspaper cutting from her wellington. "Weeding is such a satisfying business," she quoted, "as therapeutic as an outing with with axe or saw, that we should all engage in it regularly. A little and often should be the principle."

Petunia was silent for a few moments as we wandered down to a bank of Sweet William. "You see the state of mind?" she at length asked, in a whisper. "Would we tolerate this kind of aggression if it were children? And are not weeds equally innocent, fragile and lovable?"

So speak up for flowers and for weeds. Join Flower Power now. Petunia can't do it all on her own.

I'LL GO ON, BUT DON'T CHANGE A WORD

There is a fierce row going on across the water in dramatic "circles". (Half of that theatre crowd can't walk a straight line day or night). If you haven't been "keeping up", the facts are (as follows): the estate of Samuel Beckett, late of Foxrock and Paris, has taken serious objection to a staging of *Footfalls* in London; and has withdrawn the rights for the production to play in Paris. Further(more), director Deborah Turner has been banned from directing the author *for life*.

They don't like the line taken by Ms Turner.

The row has brought up important questions. Like, should a text ever be sacrosanct? How far can you go? What rights has an author? When does Summer Closing Time come in?

I have a personal interest as you can imagine. When I am dead (and gone), this "material" of mine, or a version thereof, could be on stage or screen, keeping my wife and kiddies in filthy lucre and them not having to do a tap of work bar only dropping the royalty cheques in the bank.

Would they notice any difference from they way they live now?

Not much, I suppose. But (the thing is) could I bear to have a modernist or post-modernist construction, or even a plain deal two-by-four deconstruction put upon it? Is there a danger the simple ordinary people, ideas and notions with which my prose abounds will find themselves naked on stage, or otherwise embarrassed? Will I be misunderstood, deliberately or otherwise? Will my meanings be turned on their head, blood forced down into the brain contrary to nature?

If you thought you'd make money on it I doubt if you'd be seen complaining. They say every man has his price.

Not me. I am going to issue elaborate instructions in advance. They will have to be obeyed at all costs. A panel of decent, honest directors will be named. They will be from the old school, that of realism, honesty, straight-up stuff, respect for one's elders, value for money and no jiggery-pokery. And nobody under 45 will be allowed *attend* performances of my work, never mind direct.

After all, when I fuse word, image, light and sound into a typical sunburst of glittering prose, do you think I want it fouled up in 50 years' time by some luadramán in a fake Aran geansaí imposing on it his own disgusting vision of Roman decadence as applied to Gardiner Street re-development or arterial drainage, the class of humble but honest subjects I regularly write of?

113

I do not. *Ars longa, vita brevis*, said the poet, and how right he was. I'm not going to have people laffin at me just to satsify some young hooligan's perverted "artistic" notions or requirements.

No. My selected images of: ineluctable modality, the sound of one hand clapping, a nationhood at its own deathbed, a piano-tuner's inadvertent music, the objective correlative, the thin topsoil of social construct, the spatio-temporal world of causality that lies "out there", the unplumbed depths of human desolation, plus whatever unassuming workaday dungarees-clad existential metaphors I manage to find in the poor cellar of my imagination, mightn't be much, but they are my own.

And no one is going to muck around with them. Mark my words. Here, use this mauve Pelikan Highlighter 435, but give it back.

Because I could be famous some day. Like the poet Seamus Heaney, about whom I was reading recently. His house full of photographs of himself. His head cast in bronze by Carolyn Mulholland, painted in watercolour by Louis Le Brocquy.

Yes. Well wait till you see *my* head. Smoked in peat by Bórd na Móna. Etched in charcoal by McHenry's. Percolated in Colombian coffee by Bewleys, marinaded in virgin olive oil (first pressing) by Dolmio, submerged in brine by John West, jellied in aspic by Fortnum and Mason, plastered (in plaster) by Jimmy H. Hughes & Sons (Plasterers), embalmed (in balm) by Fanagans, and finally placed, reverentially, preserved for all time, in a small bottle of formaldehyde on the highest shelf in the Mercer Library of the College of Surgeons.

That's all in front of me of course. I have many years to go yet, God willing.

ART (AND TOM) AND THE FAMILY MAN

I was reading the other day about the poet T.S. Eliot and his first wife Vivienne and the fierce rows they had together (hard to have them apart). Out of this marital battling it seems, came some of Eliot's greatest poetry, with which we are all familiar, *The Waste Land, Love Songs of Connacht, Four Quarters* and so on.

You could get the wrong idea from this. Say you are a married man. You "enjoy" a perfectly normal relationship with your partner. All right, the odd row, voices sometimes raised in anger, but for the most a warm and vibrant atmsophere of tolerance, understanding, appreciation of each other's little foibles, agreement on household expenditure, children's schooling and so on.

But say you are also a man of modest literary pretension. And the next thing is, you read about Tom Eliot and his wife. You have now (inadvertently) placed yourself on the verge of what some writers would call a powderkeg situation. It could ignite easily at any time. *What I am saying is you might easily be tempted to provoke terrible rows with the wife in order to stimulate the artistic output, if you see what I mean.*

It could lead to trouble.

Of course if your artistic output isn't as good as you think it should be, there's no harm at all in taking a good look at your domestic situation. Maybe it is true that you have things too soft. You have possibly "grown" complacent. Even your muse is putting on weight, ha ha. But does that mean you should deliberately stir things up with the wife, provoking a savage argument just so that you can produce – yes, out of the emotional upset, the soul-churning experience, the gut-wrenching interchange, the spiritual angst, the vortex of passion, the psychic catharsis and the good old-fashioned real-thing can't-be-beaten Catholic guilt – one great poem?

The central question here is, would it be worth it?

One great poem, and I am talking now of something along the lines of *The Lake Isle of Innisfree,* or *Paradise Lost,* is worth a lot of suffering is the way many would look at it, but your wife might not agree if it is she who has to suffer. (If you warn her in advance of course, all bets are off).

It is a hard question and if it is one you (yourself) never have to face you should count your blessings. Here, borrow my calculator.

Of course, the other killer in the literary world is compromise. You have to have think only of your art if you want to get on. Look at any great artist. Ask yourself. Did they ever compromise? You will find not. Tolstoy?

Joyce? Leonardo Givenchy? *The art always came first.*

So. Never mind the pale brow of your fevered and emaciated child, the blank eyes of your consumptive wife coughing her guts out in the corner, the neighbours pounding on the walls due to the noise from your typewriter. You are on line fifteen of the greatest sonnet ever written – all you need is a word to rhyme with phlogopite – and you ask should you stop, reconsider, and attend to these pitiful domestic distractions, thus jeopardising your art?

If you do, don't count on posterity thanking you, because where art is concerned, it couldn't care less about human considerations. That's the way it works, unfortunately.

The hard thing is for a family of a literary man to appreciate this and bear its suffering in the manner of the stoics.

Hold on. Here's a "scenario". what if Tom Eliot and Vivienne were alive today, with therapists and counsellors analysing them and curing their problems and so on? Result: a happy couple, but no great poetry, only doggerel that you might pick up for loose change off Aungier Street, or else saccharine drivel, *April not a bad month* and the like. Go on, strike while the iron is hot, carry on with this stuff, develop it, *Prufrock's Lovesong* with happy ending, 800 words of marvellous whimsy, flog it to the newspapers, get yourself a reputation as comic writer, detached observer of humanity's foibles, sly, wry, dry, pithy wit, always in demand the light touch in an age when papers are full of horror and evil, sees lighter side of things, refuses (who asked?) to take life seriously, goes along (happily) with theory life there to be enjoyed.

But you grow through pain, *per ardua ad astra* is what the man said.

HIP HOP, GANGSTA AND THE HEY DORIS FACTOR

I see where an album of Gregorian chant by a Benedictine order of monks has entered the Top Ten in the UK, and has taken the number one "slot" in the classical charts. The monks, from Silos in Spain, are keeping quiet, however. If they were genuine celebrities I suppose you would say they were "maintaining" a low profile.

The media love a mystery and we are falling over ourselves, clumsy folk that we are, in efforts to explain the "phenomenon" of chanted song in a hopelessly foreign language (Latin) selling more than songs with genuine English lyrics and titles like *Wa Wa Shove Your Lovin' On Me* and other indie hip hop hap-rap funk gangsta techno-house sub-acid classics like *Your Fist, My Mouth* from groups like En Vogue, Soul Asylum, D:Ream, The Wonderstuff, Take That, Worlds Apart and Salt 'n' Pepa.

Aren't you very well up on the "pop scene"?

Not really. But I am (nothing if not) meticulous in my research.

Anyway, a Mr Paul Gambaccini of EMI Records, producers of the chant, has offered his own explanation to eager hacks sussing out the phenomenon. "It has what every company dreams of - the 'What is That?' factor."

Here is what he means. You are listening, let us say, to the Gay Byrne show while ironing away (away where?), and on comes a nice piece of Gregorian chant. You stop what you are doing and as the iron burns a hole in your Marks and Spencer shirt, full cotton buttondown, the only one that "goes with" your turquoise tie, you say, looking hard at the radio, "What is that?"

EMI has you by your credit card. You will not stop until you find this record, buy it, play it, and get all your friends to do the same.

There are more of these "factors" about, and damned useful they are too for journalists who, scorning their often rural origins, and the grim but dogged reality of the grandfather's 30-year stint in the sewers of Cricklewood and Camden Town, will have nothing to do with "digging" for facts, or for anything else.

For example: I was reading about that TV programme *The Word* recently, the one where they shove in, by way of diversion, something really disgusting, like a person eating a worm sandwich. And people watch it. Why? Well, a TV executive explained that it has the "Hey Doris" factor. Do you understand, or will I spell it out? All right, I realise you are busy, and the truth is I have little else to do with my time.

It means a fellow is watching TV, the usual inconsequential run-of-the-mill stuff – murders, rapes, lootings, beatings, theft, arson, car crashes, etc., when up pops the worm-sandwich eater. The near ga-ga viewer lifts himself momentarily from his crispstrewn beer-can-surrounded grime-encrusted armchair torpor and, with a superhuman effort, spurred only by charity and that strange desire to share human experience however odd, calls out to his life's partner, who we have to presume is in the kitchen (and not making sandwiches for the supper, one prays): "Hey Doris!" Followed quickly by something like – and I can only guess at the level of familiarity, colloquialism and transatlantic influence in your own particular domestic set-up – "Get a loada this guy!"

And in trots (or pads, if you want to think of her as over 14 stone) the compliant Doris to see, and offer her comment on, the latest contribution by television to world understanding. "Gee Will, isn't that somethin'?"

And that is the "Hey Doris!" factor which so delights TV programmers. But of course it is always nice to hear of a couple sharing a cross-cultural experience.

Talking about television, I saw a fellow going on about the Holocaust recently, in connection with some film, *Swindler's List* I think it was called, and telling us that "we are all to blame." Well, he is wrong. What he says is arrant nonsense. I had nothing to do with the Holocaust. I bear no blame whatsoever. Nor had I anything to do with Attila the Hun's ravages; the selection of the World Cup team; the fall of the Roman Empire; the choice of holiday destination by our beloved President; the pollution of the Dodder; the resurgence of measles, or this intemperate Easter weather.

I will take blame when I am clearly in the wrong. Otherwise not. There must be other people like me in this respect. What is it that unites us? Yes, it is the "Had Enough" factor.

Silent Majority Speaks Out as Gaeilge

This business of inaccurate road signs in the Irish language is getting out of hand. The mood of the country is getting very dangerous. People have *had enough.*

Soundings have been taken. The pulse felt. The silent majority is on the verge of breaking its long and dignified silence. At every crossroads, the grass roots move as one, rippling in the breeze, whispering: a limit to what people will take; time come to take a stand; if we don't speak out, who will.

Yes, incorrect and misspelt Irish signs are one of the great scandals of our times. Good on ye, Éamon Ó Cuív, FF TD for speaking out on the (crying) need for Irish signs in accessible, easily understood language "and not written in dense bureaucratic terminology".

Politician calls for clear language. Media alerted, front pages held. Doctors, specialists in newropsychology – that oldro-psychology is no use at all any more – called in. Politician apologises, makes emotional statement to press. Charitable nature of Irish public asserts itself, poor fellow forgiven, could happen anyone, man's personal life is his own, let him who is without sin etc.

But there will be hell to pay for this. "Dense bureaucratic terminology" indeed – the cheek of him. Union of Dense Bureaucrats up in arms.

Fair-play-to-him-all-the-same, Eamon has gone on record with what he considers a good example of a "successful" sign, "clocha beaga scartha", a sign used to designate (*designate*, if you don't mind, is there anything else a sign might be doing and it not too busy maybe?) loose chippings in Connemara. Such a translation was better, said he, than using a direct translation of the word "chippings".

Right. We will not delay. Put this to the test right away. Crowd into the car. Shureanny excuse to visit Connemara. Out through the City of the Tribes, foot down, straight on to Moycullen, note glories of Ross Lake on right, on to Oughterard, Maam Cross – stop for pint of plain and good feed of sandwiches in Peacock's – then, thus fortified, all the way to Leenaun, where road meets bog – and Killary harbour, Ireland's Only Deep-Sea Inlet.

Oh, magical. Here we stand, right on the very edge of Europe – watch OUT, Seánín! For the love of God will ye stand well back, ye were nearly over that time, your mother'll *kill* me if annythin happens ye.

Majestic the only word for it. The serene beauty. The harmony of nature, the hawthorn in bloom, the rich and heavy fuchsia, the clear water below, the blue sky above.

119

But we have work to do.

There it is! Standing alone, huge EC sign in First Official Language: *clocha beaga scartha*. "Loose chippings" in the foreigners' tongue. But Lord save us, where will it end? This could be all the way to Letterfrack for all we know.

Yerrah, we'll give it a lash. Off with us, scattering great lumps of gravel up from the wheels. Seosamh says to me as we skid nearly into the bog, "I thought we'd had our *sceallóga* there for a minnit!"

Sceallóga is *chips* you see. On a menu would *designate* chips. Seosamh is playing on words, what with the *clocha beaga scartha* and all that. He has a great love of the language and a playful attidue to it, great fan of your man Joyce, can recite lumps of *Finnegans Wake* off by heart.

There are those who will say loose chippings are loose chippings in any language, and damn dangerous they are no matter what way you translate them. You could be doing only 20 miles an hour and wan of them stones could fly up and bang! Your windscreen is gone, £200 at the very least, VAT on top of it, and the shock is something terrible, glass all over the car finding bits of it for years afterwards no Hoover will get it all out you can get insurance I believe but sure no one ever expects that class of accident –

I asked you politely to keep your nose out of this article. Cuir isteach your spóca somewhere else if you must, but be quiet here or at least show some respect. We are speaking of place names and inaccuracy and the first official tongue. This is a serious business. Frivolity is out of place, as too is his bolder brother facetiousness.

It is a business so serious I may come back to it (in the future).

IS THERE A CRITIC IN THE HOUSE?

You will have noticed, if you're awake at all, how everyone is getting in on the play "reviewing" game, their names in the papers, giving out about plays or other people's opinions of them. Polly Devlin has no time for *The Bird Sanctuary*. Shivaun O'Casey kicks up an enormous fuss when her production of *The Plough and the Stars* is criticised. The letter columns are bursting with amateur critics.

Worse, the poor old professional critics are getting a terrible mauling. Their "opinions" are being thrown back in their faces. Their "qualifications" are deemed supsect. Their circumstances of conception are the subject of innuendo and back-street gossip.

Their job is not as soft as you might think. Giving out stink about dreadful plays week after week, thinking up things like "the setting had its own insouciance, like a lone daffodil impervious to its surroundings" is not as easy as it looks. You could be ten minutes working on that alone and checking on the spelling of "insouciance"

It's all right for you, the ordinary "play-goer", as you slip out before the second curtain-call (don't think the cast won't recognise you again in your sludge green anorak from the 1986 Boyers sale), speed recklessly back to your local in order to drop wife at pub, career 500 yards down the avenue, abandon car outside home, race back to pub risking heart attack, and arrive just in time for your two half-ones and pint of plain. But of course you have the last laff on the drivers who risk the breathalyser. Home you go then, settle yourselves, brief exchange of intelligent remarks re play.

"I though your one was looking well, given what she has to put up with from that husband of hers"

"You're right", says your wife thoughtfully, "but did you notice the gash on her leg?"

Yes. The ordinary, unremarkable sort of casual discourse that brings a couple closer together. Perhaps then a nightcap ("I warned that child I'd murder him if he went near the white lemonade. Ah I suppose a drop of water then"), News Headlines, Time Out, a Short Pause for Reflection (where did I leave that mirror), glass of milk, digestive biscuit and a warm bed. *Ah Mary! The last thing I told you was to switch the blanket on!*

That's you and your pals and your good night out at the theatre.

Next morning, you are in your office. With forgiveable smugness you remark that you "took" the wife to the theatre last night. Or you "took in" a play, even if you never understood (or were meant to understand) a word of it.

You are a man of casual culture worn easily on your broad shoulders and people show you some respect.

Now, consider the poor critic. Is usually known by sight to all in the theatre. Subject of begrudgery as a result of his miserable free ticket or two. Feels he must attack play/playwright/theatre/manager/Arts Council/Government in order to assert "independence" of viewpoint. Expected to arrive sober and stay more or less that way. Has to return directly to near-deserted office and "file copy", i.e. write at least superficially literate piece about the ludicrous fantasy he has just seen and hand it over to sub-editor who only wants to get to pub/bed and cares not at all if it appears under the Farm Machinery For Sale column or obscuring the top half of a lingerie ad.

But the playwrights have to take some blame too. Look at the titles of some "modern" plays. Frank McGuinness has a thing called *The Bird Sanctuary*. I can tell you now (for nothing) that there is very little in it about our feathered friends. I understand the bird-fancier would have been similarly let down by Cheg Ov's *The Seagull*. And God help the poor play-goer hoping for a bit of Red Indian action and maybe a tomahawk killing or two in Bernard Farrell's *The Last Apache Reunion*: he will be very disappointed.

This is symbolism (of course). Content of play nothing to do with title. But why not? Did Shakespeare carry on like that? He did not. *The Merchant of Venice* – what's that about? What it says. Did Shakespeare ever think of calling *Hamlet* "Frog Spawn on the Moon"? If he did, you can bet the wife knocked that idea on the head straight off. *The Taming of the Shrewd? Some Like it Hot?* Every one of his plays is about what they say they're about, and no nonsense.

WHEN THE DARK COW LEAVES THE MOOR

I see where some species of Irish farm animals are now endangered or almost extinct. There are only 300 original Galway sheep left, only 500 Kerry cows and hardly any original Roscommon sheep.

Emigration, I suppose. No jobs, no social life, no prospects. Sure young Frankie Ledwidge, God rest him, saw it all coming, and that was neither today nor yesterday. *He shall not hear the bittern cry.* Fair play to you Frank, you were on the ball there, devil the bittern you'd hear at all these days and you picking your way through the farmlands of Meath. *Nor voices of the sweeter birds above the wailing of the rain.* No, nothing bar an oul' crow or two cawing away in the downpour, that's what we're reduced to.

Ah, never mind. Help is at hand – and money, begob. There is a new thing called the Irish Genetic Resources Conservation Trust.

But here: look at the small print. The big Galway sheep is on its last legs because farmers discovered they could keep two smaller ewes on the same amount of land, and collect two European Union (Ewenion?) Ewe Premiums where once they could only collect one. The same is true of the Roscommon breed.

There is no limit to the ingenuity of the Irish farmer.

Scene: North Roscommon. A hill farm, maybe 60 acres, every inch of it the colour of ebony, undulating strangely, as if moving beneath a huge black velvet carpet. Peculiar squealing noises fill the air. Farmer O'Connor, a man of about average height for a Neanderthal homunculus, emerges to greet Ewe Premium Inspector.

Inspector: *Lord save us, Farmer O'Connor, you have a fierce mink infestation problem here.*

Farmer: *Mink, what mink? Them lads is it? Them is the new Roscommon ewe, specially bred be me friend Tom Crogger over beyont in Dromanahy follyin' on his £295,000 grant from the gintlemen of the Irish Genetic Resources Conservation Trust, God bless them and preserve them.*

Inspector: *And I could hardly get up your boreen for all the rabbits.*

Farmer: *Rabbits? What rabbits? I hope 'tisn't to me genetically created Roscommon Aquitaine you're referring, is it?*

Of course the farmers are having a hard time. Awful weather. Fodder shortages. Livestock wiped out by wind and hail and snow. So we read that inspectors have been asked to take a "sympathetic" approach to farmers where ewe numbers were below those claimed for when inspections took place.

Scene: The Golden Vale. A balmy breeze plays over the lea, larks are up to their usual frolics, frolics up to their usual larks, pale sunlight streams down on undulating meadowland, and all's well with the world. An inspector makes his way up a gravel drive, hides his humiliated Fiesta between a Range Rover and a Toyota Landcruiser.

Inspector: *Now Farmer Jones, you claimed for 67,895 ewe premiums.*

Farmer: *I did, I did. Will ye come in for a cup of tea, or maybe something stronger?*

Inspector: *I was out counting your herd just now and I could only find nine ewes.*

Farmer: *What? Nine is it? Holy God, There was 67,895 there this very morning, before that HUGE wind picked up. God help them, they must be nearly all gone over the cliff. Óchone agus Óchone Ó, the poor crathures. What will I do at all at all?*

Inspector: *I don't know. Have you thought of auditioning at the Abbey?*

I see too that the mushroom producers are up in arms because their "manufacturing status" is being removed, which will push up their Corporation Tax. Wasn't I the right eejit, thinking mushrooms grew in the ground, and them manufactured all along?

All right, so I haven't been living in the real world at all. Don't worry. All that's going to change. From now on this "article" will not be written, but manufactured. It will be an organic creation, environment-friendly, treated with only the safest pesticides. Naturally it will attract the top-rate EU Article Premium. That's not all. Instead of the one article, I am going to see if I can squeeze two – what am I talking about? Make that 32 pieces, shoehorned into this unique geometric phenomenon, this rectangular square: and multiply the premium until rich beyond a farmer's dreams.

STATEMENTS FROM THE USELESS DATA BANK

I see where the London *Times* has been running a sales campaign wherein they print comments from (and even photographs of) the people who have seen the light, i.e. new subscribers. "Why They Choose the Times" is an absolute darling of a little singlecolumn panel, discreetly ruled off and complete with underlines and bold dots and highlighting so on, a thing to bring joy to the hearts of designers everywhere, a (veritable) model of its kind.

Recently, the panel featured a husband and wife team, Michael and Enid, who had started "taking" *The Times* after "becoming disillusioned" with *The Independ*ent: "There was a lot of useless information in it" said Enid. Michael added: "*The Times* gives fair reporting. I start at the front and work through..."

Devil the word, of course, about the fact that *The Times* has cut its price to 30p while *The Indpendent* remains at 50p.

It's a popular notion that all newspapers are out there continually scouring the country for new readers in a desperate "bid" (Do I hear 80p? On my left? 85p? Selling now at 85p) to boost subscriptions. But were Michael and Enid to live in Ireland, I would not be hopeful about recruiting them as readers of this paper. I mean who on earth, apart from Michael and Enid, buys a newspaper for its amount of "useful information"? Of what (earthly) "use" are for example the following revelations?

Problems continue to "mount" for the British entry in the Round the World yacht race.

Sprig-tinted separates make a delightful fashion statement in navy or misty blue shell tops and flowing shirts.

The new Saab 900 has been voted Import Car of the Year in Japan.

The average Dane consumes almost three times the amount of pigmeat (65.2kg) as the average Briton.

Roald Dahl once requested Robert Gotleib, the president of his American publisher Knopf, to send out "someone competent and ravishing" to buy him six dozen new pencils and post them airmail.

Shay Healy visited a rodeo in southern Texas.

Ni hé lá na gaoithe lá na scolb.

Enjoyment is the buzz word among the players, who point to Venables' engaging blend of tactical nous and good humour as the most noticeable difference between the new regime and the old.

Uzbekistan's Djamolidin Abdoujaparov won the third stage of the Paris-Nice cycling race at Clermont-Ferrand.

Full permission is sought for a milking parlour, holding yard, effluent collection tank and associated concrete in Robertstown.

All these pieces of information, and I say this with no small measure of pride, appeared in a *single edition* of this paper recently. And they are, I can say with equal pride, essentially useless pieces of information. Does that make them less valuable? Are they less entertaining for that? Are they to be banished from the newspaper because they do not match up to unspecified readers' drearily utilitarian requirements or demands? Well?

Questions echo across subdued hall, thousands stunned into ashamed silence, mass guilt swamps auditorium, sniffles give way to loud weeping, scenes of unrestrained emotion, audience rises to its feet as one man and with one voice cries out – No! No! No!

Thank you. As for Enid's husband – well, the kindest thing we can say is that she probably deserves him. "I start at the front and work through." What a drearily consecutive way of doing things. This is the class of fellow who would *never* have his orange juice after his cornflakes.

Irish Times readers are not like that. No. They will do Crosaire first thing, even while the spouse is weeping for a look at Personal Column Extra. They will read Weather Eye and have no regard for the possibility of it raining in the next hour or not. They will read the leaders from bottom to top. And so on. They are not tied to crass notions of "usefulness", they flee free of quotidian considerations, inhabit a superior sphere of their own, ethereal, rarefied, exhalted.

They are my kind, our kind, of readers. And God bless'em. Excuse me. Not often I cry in public.

126

When Romance Stalks the Book Aisles

I read where Americans are now apparently frequenting giant bookstores in droves (Droves, Utah, I suppose) not to purchase books, or even browse, but to meet people. For chat, it appears, possibly leading to more serious stuff. Some of these huge bookstores, especially in New York, have incorporated cafes with comfortable armchairs and free reading material.

They have, I am told, created a "scene" where once there existed only a bookshop.

Couples, I read, "fall out of cinemas and restaurants on Broadway and grab a 'lit hit' before heading home".

Why do they "fall out", don't you wonder? Are they drunk? Or have they simply lost interest in one another? No. It seems the meaning of the above is that people leave cinemas and restaurants and can't resist a free late-night read before going home.

But if they are couples why should they want to "meet" other people in this quasi-(queasi)romantic situation?

Don't ask. This is New York.

"Sharon Stein, a scriptwriter, comes to the Broadway superstore about once a week and notes that she has had two offers of a cup of coffee from browsers in the drama section – and *a number of significant glances*."

In New York, mind, there are two single women to every man.

Would I cope there? (I ask myself). Would I be able to recognise a "significant" glance and know what to do about it? Me (or is it I?) No chance.

No. I will stick here in Dublin where things have their own logic, perverse, perverted, converted, insane, inane or arcane as it may be.

The aforementioned Ms Stein believes there isn't as much pressure in a bookstore as in a "singles" bar. (Would they never chance a double, say if it was near closing time? Apparently not). If you meet a fellow in a bookstore "you know he can read, which is always useful in a guy; you know he likes books. I look at it like this. If you want a man who drinks, go to a bar. If you want a man who reads, go to a bookstore."

Hasn't Ms Stein a fiercely linear approach to things, and her a scriptwriter? You could be sure the body would always turn up in the end if she wrote a thriller. In the library, I suppose.

The reporter also told how another young woman favours the poetry section in her search for a sensitive man. "Anyone reading Walt Whitman is always a good bet."

I suppose if a sensitive man is what you want, you could do worse than a devotee of Walt, who wore tights in bed and ate prune sandwiches. Not my type, though. I guess I hang out in the wrong bookstores but – I beg your pardon, I have been carried away with the New York idiom. I will start again: perhaps I frequent the wrong bookshops but the men I see there are not the type I would recommend.

As for pubs, the main risk is of meeting poetry "lovers" and their Rilke, beg pardon, their ilk. But this linkage of sociology and poetry and pub types is a study in itself. You should take a look at my monograph on the subject, which I will develop into a stereograph in good time.

There are dangers (involved). A woman could find herself hopelessly attracted to a book-lover (I suppose he would bookworm his way into her affections, ha ha) and find she has to put up with the fellow's addiction for ever. The confirmed "reader" can have nothing much done for him. (Of course it's the first page he shouldn't have).

And some books are stronger than others. You could have two pages of Roddy Doyle on an empty stomach and feel no effect. On the other hand you could have half a paragraph of Joe O'Connor as a "harmless" aperitif and be instantly on your ear, embarrassing the entire party and making sure you are never invited back. The thing is to pace yourself, and not mix genres. Otherwise you're asking for trouble.

You have the idea now, write the rest yourself, go on, grab a whisk, beat it until you have it standing up in peaks. I'm tired.

COPING WITH THE SAFARI SET

We are becoming great people for the travel. The days of the annual four days in the Isle of Man are well gone of course. We're too good for that now. Nothing will do us but places like Barbados, the Virgin Islands, "long-haul" stuff like Australia and Thailand and Keyna "safari" trips. Is it just me or do you (too) find it hard to visualise a group of our fellow-countrymen and women, most of whom were grateful for the week in Ballybunion when they were children, oohing and aahing over antelope, rhinoceros and the like "in the wild" as if they were well used to it, and blathering on about the "glories" of Tree Tops?

It can become irritating.

And where did you go on the holidays? asks your acquaintance.

Oh, camping in Curracloe, same as usual. Sez you without thinking. *And yourselves?*

We grabbed a couple of weeks in Kenya, actually.

What purpose does the word "actually" serve (in this context)? Are these people afraid they won't be believed? The "couple of" is good, though. Draws attention to last-minute holiday choice, busy man, can't be bothered with brochures, unable to fix holiday times in advance, nature of business too important, leaves everything to wife, bar Amex signature. Same thing with "grabbed". Busy busy busy you see.

Anyway you are left feeling pretty sick. But your torture has only begun.

Got good weather did you? Says your smooth friend. He knows well that the rain poured down solid last "summer", guesses (correctly) that your family was nearly washed away, tent and all, that your wife swore never again.

Middling, you hear yourself say, cursing yourself for a liar, a hypocrite, a person of hopelessly inadequate moral fibre. *Middling.* For God's sake, man.

But you can't stop now. There is a tide in the affairs of men that will make you follow up with *And yourself? Hot was it?*

Your friend laughs. "Derisively" is how those cheap novellas would put it (Well what class of adverb would you expect for your 80p?).

What's coming? Yes. The pal and his family *sweltered in ovenlike heat, absoultely incredible, 110° in the shade.*

You can't stop yourself. *A bit hard to take, was it?*

Oh well of course the villa was air-conditioned.

Did you think for a moment it would have been otherwise? No. You just didn't think at all, though you have been in this situation before.

So it goes on. Your pal is delighted to admit he (himself) went to Curracloe years ago *when the kids were young*. You know he knows your three big lumpy sons are now in their thirties and and you are *still* stuck with Curracloe.

Listen: here is how you handle it. Say you hadn't time for a holiday. Then milk all the blather out of him straight off. When he gets to the bit about the air-conditioned car, fire off your opening shot: *I suppose the beach was air-conditioned too?*

This will throw him, because most of these people are thicker than double-ditches in Tipperary North.

Pardon?

Already the tic is moving on his left cheek. You continue. *Air-conditioned. The beaches.*

Well no (nervously).

Ah. You were on the east then (Don't pause). *No air-conditioning in the beach lodges either? You must have done the old Mombasa-Nairobi rabbit run, right? Very nice of course we were there a few years back found it a bit touristy I must say so we headed* (headed is good) *up round Lake Turkana before going back over to Kisuma, edge of Lake Victoria you know, and then on to Kirinyaaga, is it called Mt Kenya now? Yes on the way back we managed to nip across the border to a typical Tanzanian village – Kyanawusteru – know it? No? Amazing culture practically untouched by civilization the Inkawathur tribe held a dinner in our honour first time I've had broiled open-sewer tiger-rat not bad at all actually they were conducting their annual manhood initiation rite quite something to watch they amputate the left ear and plunge red-hot needles into the abdominal walls you knew that of course?*

THE SPIRIT IS WILLING, THE FLESH ABSENT

I see where the latest trend in the film business is the publication of "tie-in" books which explain any of the loose ends left in the movies. If you wondered why Ada was mute in *The Piano*, for example, or why she sends a written love message to an illiterate lover, the book of the movie now reveals all.

And what, I ask (myself) will we gain from this tying up of loose ends, this modern mania for neatness and finished business? What but the reining in of the imagination, the spirit brought down from its soaring arc, the golden realms of poetic possiblity closed off, leaving us at the end of the day with nothing but a collection of pathetic oul' facts, miserable things that you wouldn't throw to a dog.

If you have something worth saying will you spit it out.

Right. What I'm getting at is this business in movies of presenting people without one or other (or more) of their faculties, and all the more heroic for it, who rise above their circumstances, their physical or mental disabilities, and create within their cruelly circumscribed world a harmonic universe –

Any hope of you getting to the point?

I mean like your man Daniel Day Lewis in *My Left Foot*. Or what's his name, yes Al Pacino, blind as could be in *Sent Off, a Woman*, and that fellow in *Rain Man*, Dustin Hoffman –

We only heard about some of those films, it's very hard for us to get into town of an evening, by the time the dinner is over and the children ready for bed and so on, sure you know yourself what family life is like, but we have your drift.

Good. Now in every one of those movies the main character had a serious disability of one kind or another. A part of him is left out so to speak. So here's my idea. I am prepared to offer my services in a movie where I will literally act myself *completely* out of existence from beginning to end. It may be an adventure story, a romance or a thriller. Either way I will serve as the focal point, the central character, even though the filmgoer will never see me on the screen at all!

We don't get you.

It is my spirit, you see, and my spirit alone, which will inform the particular film. There will be no physical back-up at all.

We have it! You mean like in Ghost, *with Patrick Swayzee! That was mighty! The sister seen it three times, bawled her head off for hours on the bus home.*

You are not far off the mark, as it happens. But *Ghost* fell at the first hurdle, you see. Your man Swayzee, dead (and all) as he was, came back. In fact he was hardly ever off the screen, no way you can keep a fine-looking fellow like him out of sight, pointless really from a director's point of view. No, he would not be at all suitable for the project I have in hand.

But yourself, not being a screen hunk, will be grand for the job, is that it?

You are getting the idea, though I do not care for your insinuations.

All we meant was you're not in the Swayzee league for looks, going by the drawing.

That is true enough, though the accompanying illustration hardly does me justice. My cheekbones are in reality better defined, the line of the lips somewhat sterner, the forehead too –

Could you hold the forehead for some other time? We haven't all day.

All right. The idea is that the viewer will never see me at all on screen, yet my presence will fill his – or her – imagination.

We won't see you in the film at all?

No. My physical presence will not register even momentarily, but spiritually, I shall completely dominate the viewing experience. If it is a thriller, my absence will terrify, will hang over the auditorium like a pall; a romance, and the pathos infused, the intangible offscreen yearning created by my wraith-like spirit, will have many in tears.

It sounds a dicey class of caper. Will you get paid?

Why shouldn't I? Absolute emotional and psychic immersion in the role will be required in order to successfully project my screen character without the aid of a visible physical presence. It is likely to be the most draining experience since the Moy.

Well good luck. I hope you're blessed with a decent director, that's all we can say.

LOOKING THE GIFT HORSE IN THE GOB

I see where American writer Alice Walker was recently pleased to be named a "state treasure" by California's arts council – but took exception to the actual award: a gilded statuette of a naked female torso. The author, whose latest book apparently deals with some unspeakable form of female mutilation, saw the statue of an "armless legless woman" as an insult to her gender.

Hold on. Hilarious teaser: If a man is 'armless and legless is he then a torso? Not necessarily – he may be just an amiable drunk!

Ah well. But what would Ms Walker have preferred, then? Something "whole, natural and non-threatening," she said. Such as? "A feather found in the forest, a seashell or a stone."

I know it's the thought that counts but personally I would be a long time thinking (and counting) before putting feathers or seashells or stones on my gift list (for receipt or delivery).

Say you are coming home after a HD at the O (yes, yes, hard day at the office, have I to spell out e-v-e-r-y-t-h-i-n-g for you?) and at the last minute, omigod, you realise it is the wife's birthday. Quickly you flit to the nearest forest, or stretch a point and just find a handy clump of trees. You scratch about, yes, you are in luck, here's a chicken-feather, not altogether fresh but (sure) you can't have everything.

You have saved the day. Your step lightens, a weight is lifted from your mind. But is your wife delighted with your thoughtfulness? Will you get a "Darling! You remembered!" and hugs and kisses and your hot dinner?

I don't think so. I very much doubt if there will be any use in you pointing out that this feather (or stone or seashell) is unique, individual, hand-picked, *sui generis*, alone of all its kind. If your spouse is any way materialistic at all (and why wouldn't she be, where would the two of you be if there wasn't one sensible one in the family, certainly not in your 4-bed semi-d out there in the Rathfarnham foothills, Mazda in the drive, master bed *en suite*, patio furniture and maybe the conservatory next spring if you cash in the policy early) she will have little time for this sort of thing.

There is one "scenario" wherein (do you like "wherein"?) your stones and feathers and seashells may be acceptable. Here it is, ate it up while it's hot. You are young, madly in love, you are, yes, new age hippies, with flowing cheesecloth dresses, tie-died shirts, beads, flowers in the hair, the lot. If that's the case, seashells and the like are fine, you will treasure them forever until you grow up and get sense and drop your unsuitable long-term partner and marry a banker.

Then you will look back and laugh at what a romantic you were, so young, so idealistic, so adventurous, so vital, so full of *joie de vivre* and of course so very much in love.

It's easy for you to be cynical but we wouldn't be surprised if you were one of them hippies yourself once, you have a short memory.

Not that short. But that was neither today nor y.

And this business of receiving awards and honours is tricky. You can't be pretending you don't deserve something for your efforts, but you have to be modest too. Look at John Gielgud at 90 – the more modesty, the more awards. That's the way to do business of course. Look at Garbo, I want to be left a loan, and was she ever short of a few bob in all her reclusivity? I doubt it very much.

The ultimate award is – nothing. Can you imagine the incomparable glory of standing up on the podium and graciously accepting, from your dearest admirers, your many chums too numerous to mention, this wonderful tribute, this, this nothing; this zero, this cypher, this negative, this absence, this transcendent vacuum, this intangible nullity, this essence of nihilism, this apogee of negation.

The fellow coming up after you for his trophy or even his feather (from the forest) will look a right eejit as he waves it about foolishly (or even foolishly about).

You on the other hand have nothing to take attention away from your casual talent, your guileless charm, your flashing dimple, your deep-cleft chin, your aquiline features, your deft wit, your endearingly old-fashioned turn of phrase, your humble, humble self.

DUST THOU, ART, AND DO IT PROPERLY

Nothing much doing today, just a couple of ould scenarios I found threwn down in the basement, dust something fierce down there, where does it all come from? No I mean really, apart from that Sahara stuff, *where does dust come from?* I often ask myself that, never mind what is the moon and the stars it's the dust that causes more problems than anything else, and why does it *settle*, I mean it can't be just to help out the novella writers where would they be without biting the dust, when the dust settled, dusted himself off, heat and dust, why does some of it stay in the air, the rest *settle*?

Yes, and where does dust go when you have done the dusting? Do you think it is all carefully enclosed in Mrs Mildew's duster on her Tuesday and Friday morning visits? If so you are more naive that I give you credit for (usual 30-day arrangement, heavy penalties for overdues, Final Demand in big red capital letters, scare daylights out of you, after that the sheriff at the door, all the neighours looking on, the shame of it).

Then this ignoble business of slopping water about to "keep the dust down". And why not let it up and about, why this cruel repression, this unworthy human desire to subdue, in dust's nature to rise like yourself and family, make its own way in the world, some of it wants to sit up there on the wardrobe, the picture frames, cling to the ceiling and why wouldn't it? And what did poor Arthur do to be landed with that class of work, job to be done over and over again, dust thou, Art, and in to dust thou shalt return indeed.

There you are now Mags, 50-odd lines on dust alone, straight off, a tenner at five to one, that's fifty and my own ten back, sixty in all, you won't make bets like that again in a hurry, ha.

Anyway. I nearly forgot the scenarios I rooted out, a bit more room in the basement now thank God.

Here's wan: From all corners of the world, reports are – yes – pouring in, all of North America entirely ablaze, South America nearly as bad, Australia burning up from left to right, blaze fanned along by fierce winds, Asia too lighting up the night sky with fire still breaking out at thousands of new points, all of Europe burning furiously, Africa one vast bush fire, millions of people running for their lives, entire world one immense inferno, non-stop screaming, homes demolished, dead and wounded everywhere, people rushing to the ocean, tragedy on massive scale, flights to Arctic Circle booked out, ice-floes melting in Greenland, smoke hanging in giant palls far as the eye can see, volcanoes reactivated, earthquakes rocking entire continents, flames rising higher and higher, worldwide panic, heat affecting earth's tectonic plates, earth's surface baked to a hideous black crust.

But wait! Detective Hodgins of Scotland Yard is at hand. He has lost every-thing in the fire, wife, kiddies, home, left arm and best workday suit. Suspects arson. Months of patient sorting through worldwide rubble, sifting charred remains, searching for clues. And gets his man. Yes. Slowly, care-fully, relentlessly. Gets to know him, his family, background, patiently works away till Paddy breaks down. Go on Paddy, tell me, I know it was your mother's fault, but what did she say, what drove you over the edge with your bottle of petrol, what did she say about you in front of your best pals, humiliating you, go on, you're only telling me what I already know, come on now –

"She said, she said –"

Easy there Paddy. Spit it out. It'll do you good.

"She said – poor old Paddy will never set the world on fire."

And you wasting good money on joke books.

Wipe your eyes, I have another:

No, sister, don't be tryin to comfort me, I can't stand it anymore, the whole thing getting me down, life what does it mean are we just floating specks in an uncaring universe, no visible purpose being served why am I flaying me guts out, life slipping away, well into second half of life now, who cares and what does it all mean in the long run, nothing at all –

There there brother, don't carry on so –

I will if I want to. Almond I as entitled as anyone else to my midlife cry, sis?

PROPERTY THEMES GIVEN THE RUNAROUND

I was talking to this house the other day –

Bear with me AAAAAAAAAAAAGH.

It's all right, he's gone now. Look them in the eye and they'll back off they're not dangerous really it's the American Brown Bear you have to watch out for, the Irish Pink species wouldn't touch a fly (but then you're not a fly, are you?).

Will we get any sense out of you this morning at all?

That remains 2B seen. What I'm getting at is – when the property pieces are being written up are houses ever consulted? If not why not?

For example: you read that a house "enjoys fine views of the sea". Do you think the house (in question) ever been asked its opinion? Maybe it *hates* sea views. Maybe it is dying to live in the country, shake the city dust off for ever, settle down in a pretty village overlooking the green sward, forge close bonds with its neighbours, live out its old age in an unutterably rustic idyll. So why these patronising and perhaps libellous imputations?

I don't know. But wouldn't you like to read (just once) that "This house is quite bored with its views"? Or "The house puts up with views of the sea". Or "This house has no time at all for its southwesterly aspect".

And what about these people who have their house designed to "reflect their own personalities."?

Hold on. Scenario coming up.

Architect: Well, what do you think?

Young Newly-Wed Woman: It, ah, looks a bit, well, dull.

Architect (brightly): Yes it does doesn't it?

Young Newly-Wed Man: It has a kind of, em, hangdog look about it. Looks rather, well, boring.

Architect: Yes. I'm glad you can see that, that's what I was aiming for. But don't you see a certain naive innocence in it too, a foolish confidence in life, a sort of daft optimism reflected in the gable end?

YNWM (unhappily): I suppose so.

Young woman bridles, nudges husband to make him "assert" himself. It works. (Remember they have not been married very long, ha ha).

YNWM (firmly): Well actually we expected a bit more formality in the reception area, perhaps a less minimalist look in the bedroom, we thought some large framed areas might enhance the jagged symmetry of the landing and that the kitchen might, you, know, *flow* a bit more into the patio area...

Architect (losing patience): I think you'll have to admit I worked exactly to your brief.

YNWM and YNWW: You did?

Architect: I have it here in writing. "More than anything we want our new house to reflect our personalities."

The contract is signed, there's nothing they can do. They have learnt a hard lesson.

A fellow was writing in this paper recently about some fine design items in a particular house. He came to the bathroom: "A pipe emerged through the floor by the side of the bath and I thought – what courage to allow the chimney flue from downstairs to travel up exposed."

Indeed. You can picture the designer (I'd do it myself but I'm in a hurry, mother-in-law coming round any minute now, this ether is useless) psyching himself up, pulse racing, must be brave, but screws his courage to the sticky place and he'll not fail.

By the way if you ever go mad and get a "theme" into your house you will find it a lively yoke. Consider the busy itinerary of a recent "classical" theme in the *Irish Times* property pages. What did it do and it barely in the door? Ran right through the house. After that? We can only hazard a guess. Out through the back door I suppose, down the garden, away (with it) up the lane, out on to the Rathmines Road, no stopping until it gets all the way down to South Richmond street, finally out of breath at the Bleeding Horse and staggers in for a well-earned pint.

Them themes would wear you out.

TIME TO RENEW YOUR SEXUAL LICENCE

I see Aer Lingus spending (good) money on telling us in large advertisements how careful an eye they keep on their planes – "even with 200 flights to 30 places, we can still tell you precisely where all our aircraft are at any given moment."

And you thinking a big bulky thing like an aeroplane would be hard to lose.

Hold tight now, seatbelts on, we are going to be flying about a bit, lots of interconnected scenarios, you will need to stay awake.

Scene: Quickfly Airlines.

Manager: *Mary! Come in here! Where's our pink and blue Airbus, is it over in America or what?*

Mary (a demure lowslung creature from three miles outside Tralee): *Is it Chucky? Arrah take it easy Mikey, sure it must be somewhere.*

Cut.

High in the Himalayas, the remains of a pink and blue Airbus shine brightly against the snow. Seven survivors stagger to their feet. Some 300 other unfortunate travellers and crew lie scattered in pieces from Tibet to Katmandu. After long and agonized discussion, the seven draw straws: it is poor Myles Hardblain who will be that evening's dinner.

Cut.

Manager: *Mary! Any news?*

Mary: *Michael, there isn't sight nor sound of it. Where could it be at all (at all)?*

Cut.

Back in the Himalayas: Maureen, a quiet, firm-hippped woman of middle years, moves purposefully towards Myles.

Myles (nervously): *Surely it can't be dinnertime already?*

Maureen: *No, it is but the cocktail hour. Myles, have you faith?*

Myles: *I have.*

Maureen: In the Lord God?

Myles: *No, the Quickfly small print. See – "Even with 576896 flights to 8765 destinations, we still have a pretty good idea of where any plane is at any given time, within reason of course."*

Maureen (grimly): *Dinner will be at 7.30 pm sharp.*

Cut.

Mary is going on her lunch hour now, meeting Jim, her fiancé, in Clery's rooftop restaurant. They will talk about their new house, their honeymoon in Barbados, flight courtesy of Quickfly. May the Lord look after them.

We think this stuff is running out of steam, or aviation fuel maybe.

You are right. Okay. Hold on now. I'm going to try a difficult piloting manoeuvre, a link-up to something entirely different, but so cleverly done you will hardly notice, all right, ailerons down, maneouvre accomplished, here we are, a perfect loop.

I see one of my colleagues telling the church in Ireland not to be so afraid of us journalists.

He's right. All I have to do is look out the window here, priests running past our offices in terror, nuns with police escorts, street regularly exorcised at midnight (don't think you haven't been seen, Father Moloney).

Yet as my colleague says "we (journalists) are not all the deceitful propagandists for secularism and sexual licence they often seem to believe."

No. Only some of us, no names named. But listen, have you been down to the sexual licence office recently? The queues are only shocking. Terrible understaffing of course, and the bureaucracy! Supply two recent photos minimum size 35mm x 35mm, complete form in block capitals with ballpoint pen, get guard's signature, use this form only if resident in the State, enclose "long" birth cert showing names of parents, section 2 only to be completed if birth cert name differs from that to appear on sexual licence, take your number and join the queue, children to be kept under strict control in the waiting area.

Go on, fill in the rest yourself, provisional sexual licences, licence revoked, endorsed, etc., what are you waiting for, no end of rib-tickling thigh-smacking fun and all you need is paper and pen.

OF BOOKS, LIBRARIES, CO-WRITERS AND THE TUTORIAL CIRCUMFLUENCE

A book owner has written to ask my advice on when a collection of books may properly be called a "library". Are two books sufficient? Six? How many? My correspondent's own opinion is that the number of books is irrelevant "as long as you have read one of them". I appreciate the compliment, but how can I know if I have read one (or more) of them when I have not been informed of the titles?

The truth is I cannot be of much help here. The books/library question is a notoriously thorny one, with little agreement and even less original research done on the subject. However, in recent years a general consensus has been reached in bibliography circles (I cannot speak for the quadrilaterals) that reading books has little (or nothing) to do with the issue, not to mention being a complete waste of time in this age of computers and information highways.

Would it be fair to say we are talking here not of mere differences of opinion but of polarities?

You have put your finger on it. Now please remove that rather coarse digit and allow me continue. The raw fact is that no empirical investigation has yet been initiated (never mind "carried out"). All I can do therefore is to direct my correspondent towards the two seminal works on the subject, namely Wilhelm Wurpel's fine monograph in *Vierteljahrschrift für Litteraturwissenschaft und Geistegeschichte, XXVI*, and Julia Karnstorm's *Neurosis in Our Time* (New York, 1937). On the synaesthesia aspects, one could usefully refer to Ottokar Liebfraumilsch's thoughtful exposition, *Über Verbindung von Farbe und Kland: Eine literar psychologische Untersuchung* (*Zeitschrift* für *Ästhetick, 11(1907)* pp 608-911.

All to be found in any good library, and I'm not trying to be smart (here).

Right. Now to less arcane matters. I saw a while back in our Corrs and Cla(nge)rs column (we don't stand on ceremony here, which is just as well with the dirt of the shoes on some people) where a gentleman pointed out – actually I am wrong. I think he simply *wished* to point out. We have to get this right. Hold on there till I get the thing in front of me.

Lorna! Lord save us that girl is never here when I need her. All right. I'll dig it out myself, fortunately I have a good spade with me, kept for these very emergencies.

Here it is. "Mr Terence Brown wishes to point out that his letter...was in fact co-written with Mr Colm Toibin."

Well I hope he gets his wish, that's all I can say because the Corrs and Clars column is a *very* short distance from the offices of our legal advisers, I can tell you that for nothing.

We, the newspaper, added that Mr Toibin's name was inadvertently omitted. In case you thought it was deliberately, vindictively, gleefully and/or viciously and maliciously omitted by someone with a grudge who hates the fellow's guts and cannot stand the mention of his name.

No, the omission was inadvertent. We could easily have put the whole thing in the classified columns and charged for it. Charged for it – but how? you ask in amazement. As an inadvertisement, of course. Talk to one of our inadvertisement executives, great offers going these days, two for the price of one in the birth column, die now pay later in obituaries and so on.

But I am intrigued with this business of "co-writing" a letter. Sometimes we get letters in here apparently written by hordes of people, entire committees. How do they do this? Pick a word each and appoint a co-ordinator, a *rapporteur*?

I have it on good authority that Mr Toibin is himself an eminent writer. Does he now plan (to forge) a concomitant career as an eminent co-writer? The wellknown co-writer. The young, up and coming co-writer. The promising co-writer. Will we see (a plethora of) new awards and prizes? The Irish Times Prize for Co-Writing was today awarded to. The International Fiction Co-Writing Award was made to. And will there be jealousy if there is only one medal and the two co-writers who work so well together on the (printed) page but who hate each other's guts, have to share it, six months each? What about publicity tours? Are two families to be deprived of their loved ones while the co-authors spin about in that fashionable tutorial circumfluence, the lecture circuit?

142

DAYS AT THE DÔME WITH ZELDA, EZRA AND "PAPA" EAMON

I picked up the paper the other day (people will keep leaving it on the floor) to read about about the writer Ernest Weekley, whose wife Frieda von Richtofen left him for DH Lawrence. "(Weekley) had woeful brown eyes and a droopy moustache; played golf, smoked a pipe and later in life, after Frieda. . ."

Yes, for the mature smoker, only Frieda will do. At all good tobacconists. Never mind your Condor, St Bruno, Mick McQuaid, Three Nuns of Malten, only Frieda gives that deep satisfying flavour, that lingering aftertaste –

On the other hand maybe he smoked Frieda in the manner of a salmon, or mackerel. This is frightening. And what did he smoke later in life, "after Frieda"? Nothing, it seems. He "buried himself in crossword puzzles and P.G. Wodehouse." Beats the cold damp earth I suppose.

Anyway. The stuff on Weekley illustrates (if you don't mind) an interesting new trend in the reviewing game.

Eamon Dunphy in the *Sunday Independent*, by way of commenting on Roddy Doyle's *Family*, tells us he suspects that Roddy "uses a facecloth to wash his cute little face. And wears pyjamas. And eats bran flakes. . ."

Right. Of course James Joyce had a thin face, poor eyesight and when going to bed took off his socks last thing. Makes you think twice about the value of *Ulysses* doesn't it? Throw in the fact that Jemser preferred white wine to red and sure there you are, hardly what you'd call a man's man, would you be bothered reading *Dubliners* at all?

Eamon himself (of course) sleeps in the raw, maximum four hours, up before dawn, 16-ounce sirloin steak and hominy grits for breakfast, gallons of strong black coffee, shirt slashed to the navel, *El Pais* open at the sports pages, nobody allowed speak a word while the early morning's sensory experiences are filtered –

Ah but the Paris days! Tell us Eamon, how are all the old interwar expatriate crowd, do you see them at all these days? God but will we ever forget those nights in the 'Quarter, Ezra and e.e. at the Dôme, Kiki wowing them at the Jockey Club in Montparnasse (*Les filles de camaret se disent toutes vierges/Les filles de camaret se disent toutes vierges/Mais quand elles sont dans mon lit/Elles preferent tenir ma vis/Q'un cierge – qu'un cierge – qu'un cierge)*!! and poor Ernest. But sure we all saw that coming. Or any of the Pamplona gang? Do you remember our night with Maria and Arancha when Rita Valetta danced the *zapateado* and we ate barbecued suckling pig with our fingers and the fat moon sat up there like a big ripe watermelon and

Zelda cried for happiness and lost love, signs were on her then of course and you knocked McAlmont flat with a straight left when he called Maria the "earthmover" and we went on to the Plaza del Toros and you killed three bulls at the *corrida* how the crowd cheered for "Papa" Eamon and you hammered out three thousand words sitting there in the dust for the *Saturday Evening Post* before we drank margaritas for nine days and Scott was locked up by the police?

Ah well. In those days the like of the Weekley/Doyle attacks (indeed the weekly Doyle attacks) we would't have tolerated at all, no, it was all teasing-out the noble mosaic of human endurance and survival, and personal insult wasn't fair, we'd say, nothing but an oul *argumentum ad hominem*, not like today, the classics deserted, no appreciation – as Father Anthony Meredith noted the other day, and never spoke truer word, *hic iacet lingua latina, Augustinus flet; lacrimas tu funde Gregori; quam Cicero loquitur lingua latina silet. Una voce Leo, Livius Tacitusque loquuntur; nunc post annorum millia tumbus habet.*

Bringing us back to the cold damp earth again. But where are my manners! I have forgotten all about poor Weekley, Frieda and Lawrence. Come down here, pull up a chair, this next will interest you. A sequel to *Lady Chatterley's Lover.* Yes indeed, *Lady Chatterley's Daughter.* I jest not. To be published next year by Macmillan, written by Elaine Feinstein, a biographer of Lawrence "She is a poet you see, and so was he. He would have liked her to do it more than anyone." (Sez a commentator).

Of course he would! Sure weren't we in touch with him only last month through the late Mr Leslie Flint just before he died. You did hear of his death, Leslie Flint, medium? Don't be confusing him with Leslie Flint large or small ha ha. But we'll come back to this.

144

TRIPPING OUT WITH TERENCE, THE PYSCHONAUT OF INNER SPACE

I was reading in a British newspaper the other day about a Mr Terence McKenna, 47, described as an ethno-botanist and psychedelic philosopher –

A what?

An ethno-botanist and psychedelic philosopher.

We'd say you'd be thumbing the pages of Education and Living *for mannies the long day before you'd see that come up under* Me and My Job.

I imagine you are correct.

So what's his game exactly?

Well, once every two months he gets into bed and takes what he describes as "an heroic dose" of psilocybin mushrooms.

Fried? With butter and a pinch of salt? Oh lovely.

He mentions neither cooking preparation nor procedures.

They're not those little button mushrooms that taste like aeroboard?

I think not. These mushrooms are hallucinogenic

What? Drugs!

Correct. But Mr McKenna explains: "My mind-brain system is a laboratory where I explore the great mystery of life. The boundaries that define the waking world are dissolved. I become a psychonaut of inner-space, entering complex experiences beyond language, bizarre yet beautiful landscapes never seen before."

The Lord save us. What does he think about dreams?

That each night we are trying to rediscover something we find and lose every 24 hours; that when we dream we are plunged into some primordial pool of imagery.

The kitchen scissors is the one thing we're always losing here. Listen. We dreamt last night there was this big black fellow standing over us with a sharp spear and he about to stick us with it like a pig, then we woke up swimmin in sweat. What would your man make of that?

I really couldn't say. Have you perhaps visited Africa?

No. Wait a minute. We had a week in Morocco four years ago, family room and two swimming pools, £600 all in bar the travel tax, the noise was fierce with the all-night discotheque downstairs but great value all the same. Would that count?

There might well be a connection there.

Dreams is peculiar, that's for sure. Where did you say your man lives?

California.

We're not all that surprised.

Nor I.

So it isn't a steady desk job he has, 9 to 5, weekends off, six weeks' holidays, grace day after the Bank Holiday weekends, and a pension to look forward to?

Your irony is amusing. Nevertheless. . .

He makes a living out of it all the same?

It appears so. Mr McKenna is pictured in rather an attractive room in his Californian home and also speaks of his house in Hawaii.

Begob he must be doing all right so. Is he a married man?

He and his wife have divorced after 15 years.

The poor woman, maybe she's better off. He's out at wild sex and drug orgies every night of the week I suppose?

On the contrary, he claims to be very reclusive and unsociable.

Does he take a jar?

His idea –

If a man doesn't take a jar, and there's no medical condition involved, it's a good bet he's gone mad on drugs, that's our opinion.

His idea of a great evening is, and I quote, "a 200-year-old book and a snifter of brandy".

Fair play to him. Brandy is an expensive poison. Where exactly does all his money come from?

Books, lectures, records and CDs dealing with his dreams and hallucinations.

We're in the wrong line of business is all we can say.

I am familiar with the feeling.

EPISODES, RANDOM THEMES, ART VANDALISM AND PANEL GAMES

Today's "piece" will take an episodic form. That's right. All I have going is a few bits and pieces and I will not try to disguise the fact, nor apologise for the dearth of imagination, the paucity of good stories and jokes and the emptiness of the intellectual larder long before shopping day.

Neither will any pathetically obvious attempts be made to create supposedly "linking" themes or any other superficially friendly arm-in-arm arrangements designed to draw attention away. Away from what? From the episodic nature of this piece of course, will you pay attention for goodness' sake.

No. Its structure will reflect (if I can get this cheval-glass into position, you wouldn't believe the weight of it) the episodic nature of life itself. For (as you well know) all human experience is unattached random incident, luck and ill-luck fall where they will, one cup poured into another makes different waters, tears shed by one eye would blind if wept into another's eye, the breast we strike in joy is not the breast we strike in pain and any man's smile would be consternation on another's mouth.

(Thanks, Djuna Barnes, I couldn't have put it better myself, not that I have tried, mind you).

All right. I see where the art critic in the *Telegraph*, a Mr Dorment (and what awakened his Dorment interest in art, you might well ask) giving out stink about acts of art vandalism, in particular the recent attack on the dead sheep exhibit by Damien Hirst in the Serpentine Gallery.

Now anyone who knows me knows my interest in matters artistic, so I am intrigued when Mr Dorment says that "in vandalising a work of art, the perpetrator quadruples public interest in it".

You think the fellow exaggerates? Well take a gawk at the following paragraph:

ìÄ♣¿°ªÑ$#@%)Whishty09871 #@$——° ¥ ♣ïîîkalfat wqqjmjmh♣ª
rty*vbg$ó90(0)&bn,,?hy rt♣))(o)!!!#dFGa♣ 9Utg♣f lkj":!#°cds 0-*

Isn't that a terrible sight? That's what happened when I left my desk and my keyboard unattended for an instant (coffee) the other day. My art despoiled, my train of thought derailed, mindless vandalism, act of the philistine, blind reaction of rage to the challenging, the complex, a feral desire to destroy, wipe out what cannot instantly be understood.

But what happened subsequently? When the poor vandalised paragraph was nevertheless published in all its gruesomeness, blood still pouring out of it? *Four times* as much public interest in the thing (and its "meaning") as before, that's what (and Mr Dorment vindicated). Public revulsion in liberal quarters, charitable impulses of the decent prose-reader, phones hopping, faxes buzzing, post-bag bursting. Now some of this may of course have been idle curiosity, the ghoulish element in humanity, that ugly human trait of voyeurism, gaping at the scene of the crash: but for the most part, the reaction was genuine, heartfelt.

So can I (find it in myself to) forgive the gurrier responsible? Can I understand his fear of the unknown, his dark little mind and its ratlike machinations? Of course I can, sure you couldn't buy publicity like that. Hey Billy! Pick up the unmarked banknotes at the usual spot, loose brick at the Bull Wall, sure you know it well by now.

By the way I see where new panel games are being sought by radio/tv. Alright, here's my pilot programme. Answer the following three questions correctly, put them together to make a "popular expression" and you may yet feature on the celebrity panel in the very first game:

1. Would you say Van Morrison is hard to make out?

2. Sounds like something you might eat rare with chips, or what you have to put through a vampire's heart to finish him off. What is it?

3. I carry this intangible with me (where Ayre I go, even the Scottish Highlands) and it is worth (or so they say) more than my purse and presumably its contents, regardless of the £500 in cash and vulgar drop-down display of laminated credit-cards.

Got them all? Okay. Stick them together without punctuation. First up with *I would stake my reputation* is the winner.

That should sort out the men from the Mensas, whah?

UP WITH THE BOG OF ALLEN, AND GOOD VALUE IN STEREOTYPES

It's very hard to beat a quiet Saturday morning poring over the *Irish Times* books pages. Yes, intimations of the cultured man in his drawing-room, sun pouring in over his left shoulder, wife tip-toeing in (and out) with fresh-brewed Bewley's Number Three, turning the pages to see what new delights are in print, casting a critical eye over the small but carefully chosen selection of paperbacks, chortling over the latest literary rows (friction of the week), perusing the Bestsellers list where authors discover the kind of stuff the public is interested in rather than the drivel so many of them keep on turning out, and the modest Contributors' panel with the shy little tagged-on advertisements for the critics' own humble offerings.

This is not to say there is no intellectual challenge in these pages. Far from it. You can easily get yourself into a right tizzy over the allegations and assertions, spilling your coffee on the Youghal-to-Youghal and scalding the cat. For example. I saw one of my colleagues in the Books pages musing recently on how big cities have often become central characters in narrative novels, instancing the work of Dickens, Zola and E.L. Doctorow.

Yes and quite unfair it is too. Why this snobbish social bias in favour of the metropolitan, the urban, and the (implied) cruel prejudice towards the rural, the remote, the rusticated? Let us internationalise the argument. What has the Empire State Building over Ardnacrusha – I'm talking now in artistic, aesthetic terms – what has the Tokyo Underground over the Rural Electrification Scheme other than its city grime?

I'm waiting for the book whose author will have the courage to make a memorable character out of our much-neglected central plains. ("In this distinguished debut novel, the great Bog of Allen is the masterpiece of characterisation in a beautifully realised gallery of individuals. Much more than a symbol, the Bog is a fully realised and powerful presence, dominating...")

Anyway, I have a crow to pick (or is it pluck? I can never remember) with Mr Doctorow. According to the reviewer of his book *The Waterworks*, the narrator at one point reminds his reader that there are "severe limits to a newspaperman's metaphysics."

The cheek of him. If you see him tell him to drop in any night to Doyle's or the Palace, hear my colleagues and myself quietly analyse over mature pints of plain the very latest in fully-pleated slub silk metaphysical utterance and style, observe how we shift with cool antithesis between philosophy and music, join debate on why G minor was Mozart's most personal key, wrangle over theories of quantum chromodynamics, the crude violation of parity and particle-anti-particle symmetry in – why, our conversations are nothing less than a long unfolding of meditative melody (punctuated by a sparing use of left-hand pizzicati and glissandi).

By the way. One of our reviewers was telling you recently in the books pages about a couple of reissued books by poor old Walter Macken, whose star has waned in recent years (wasn't it him who wrote the history of Irish bus conducting, *Seek the Fare Land*, or have I got him mixed up with some-one else?). Anyway the books, said our man, are embedded in the conventions of the Irish rural novel, which still flourishes *but has an entirely new set of rules and stereotypes today.*

Yes, and you can pick them up at the Government Publications Office, great value at 30p, subsidised by the taxpayer, and only right too. That's just for the rules of course, the stereotypes are a good bit dearer (rental only) but they're a dacent bunch, put them in an easy chair with a ball of malt and observe them at your leisure, they'll only speak when spoken to, very well trained of course from the old school. The least sign of trouble out of them and the lads in the white coats will be out pronto and you'll get a full refund.

Monotypes are only half the price but frankly they're a poor-looking lot, certainly the ones I've met, and you're better off going for a stereotype if you can afford them at all, it will pay off in the long run. Wouldn't you die of shame if your Irish rural novel (new variety, late flowering) was written off in the *Irish Times* as monotypical (of its *genre* need I add) and you with no comeback, details of the embarrassing transaction there in the records of the Government Publications Office for all to see?

FROM THE MILKY WAY TO KAMCHATKA

I was reading the other day about Christina Dodwell, a woman who has been travelling for over 20 years.

Travel broadens the mind and empties the pockets, that's our opinion for what it's worth.

Ms Dodwell's definition of travel is "a wonderful emptiness just waiting to be filled".

That's deep all right. What drives her at all?

When she begins dreaming that she is riding an elephant through the Milky Way, she feels this represents her unconscious goading her into action. She then packs a rucksack and flicks through her atlas, trying not to have any preconceptions about where to go.

Fair play to her, no messing around with holiday brochures and arguments over Majorca versus Ibiza. We'd be ready to bet she isn't a married lady with children?

She married three years ago but there is no mention of children.

Children can drive you cracked on a holiday, that's our experience. So herself and the husband go off together then?

No. He remains at home. Ms Dodwell believes that when travelling she needs to rely entirely on her own inner resources.

We'd say it's very hard on him all the same, but I suppose he knew what he was letting himself in for?

Ms Dodwell does say he knew that she was not going to sit in the kitchen studying new recipes.

She stays in five-star hotels all over the world I suppose?

On the contrary, she regularly sleeps out in the open, either in a sleeping bag or – when in lion country – in a hammock slung between two trees.

We were out in Texas Homecare the other Saturday, nothing would do the wife but to buy a hammock but sure the trees in the back garden aren't suitable for the job at all, when you climb in, the rear end if you'll pardon the expression is tipping the ground.

Getting the best out of a hammock certainly involves some skill.

How old did you say your one was?

I didn't. She is 43.

So does she get into any tight spots travelling on her own?

One night by the Congo river her –

Women are often at their best in their 40s is what we hear. Go on quick, what happened at the Congo?

Her camp was attacked by bandits.

Lord save us!

She had to wade through the river waters.

Were they pitch-black, crocodile-infested waters?

Your knowledge of conditions in the Congo region is impressive.

So tell us, what happened?

She says she suddenly realised she wasn't scared any more.

Why not?

She asserts there "simply wasn't time".

We'll have to think that through. Any other adventures?

Last year in Kamchatka (east of Siberia)...

We're very grateful for the parentheses.

She spent a month sleeping with six men.

What?

The temperature was minus 40 and she professed herself glad to share their tent.

Still and all.

If you are referring to sexual advances –

We never said that!

She says they have been rare.

There must have been the odd one though?

Yes. Some young men in Papua New Guinea once politely spoke to her as follows: "We hear you're alone and travelling a long way. Would you like some sex?"

That's a shocking thing to ask anyone. Did she call the police?

She asked the young men for directions instead, and no one was offended.

We'd say she got off light there.

Ms Dodwell believes that security has nothing to do with walls and houses, but is inside a person.

We wouldn't feel safe in the bed without the Chubb lock on the door all the same.

Your instinct is probably correct.

SUCCESS GOES TO THE NATIONAL HEAD

I see where the current "economic boom" is creating its own problems. We are informed that because the country is doing so well, our status as a favoured nation for EU funding is now endangered.

We're doing too well for us to be holding out the begging bowl any longer, seems to be the translation. Do you understand or have I to spell i-t o-u-t t-o y-o-u? A tramp that looks well-fed (and is well dressed and well spoken) doesn't get much sympathy in the street, that's well known. Our increased style as a nation, our standing on the world stage, our burgeoning international reputation in (the field of) art, film, sport and fashion, our headlong rush to embrace the liberal agenda, our eager sloughing off of the old ways, our casual disengagement from the songs our fathers loved – all have brought this ironic backlash.

But one commentator has suggested a solution to this dilemma of economic success undermining claims for aid. He thinks we should "ring fence" relatively prosperous regions including Dublin (though not relatively Prosperous in Kildare). Special funding status could then be claimed for poorer parts of the country.

I am all for this, and am willing to put my money an inch below my nose (where my mouth is). At this very moment I have the whole family busy in the back yard running together a good strong ring fence out of best chicken wire. We have about 200 yards strung out so far and if the weather holds we'll have that doubled by the weekend (of course concrete posts will be another day's work).

We'd be further ahead but we had to spend the Bank Holiday weekend with the in-laws and with all the chat and to be honest the drink, we got nothing much done. These decent people live a few miles outside Sneem and are deeply appreciative of our efforts, though they remain confident enough of their own status as an underprivileged area, no danger of them being cut-off from any EU funds going, they have it all well sussed and why wouldn't they.

Anyway Joseph (wife's brother-in-law) said little when all this debate was going on but thought all the more. Joseph is a great man for taking an idea one step further of course. He then pointed out it's often the case that when a will is made the poor old mother or father, in a desperate attempt to be fair to everyone, puts it in writing that the money and/or farm is to be divided equally between all the offspring. Though meaning well, the will-maker often seem to forget that just about every member of every family has different levels of wealth, with equally different needs.

Joseph's idea therefore is to "ring fence" the wealthier family members, i.e. cut them out altogether, and let the needier family offspring divide any cash or property going. He thinks any embarrassment would probably be outweighed by the cash windfall.

Personally I think this might cause more problems than it might solve. Joseph is a crack economist of course, eating Central Bank bulletins and trade surplus figures for breakfast, but the man is a bit out of touch with ordinary people and their lives. Re the will business, I contented myself with asking him, not too cryptically, who would bell the family cat, or cats. He is of a literal turn of mind and didn't get my meaning.

By the way don't be trying to ring in here between 9 and 9.15 am, it's a dead loss, this is ego-feeding time in the newsroom and there are voracious appetites to be catered for, obscene mounds of editorial praise to be shovelled out, desktops groaning with best cuts of *plámás,* the floor like a skating rink with obsequiousness, the whole place awash with oleaginous fawning and moaning and pleading, interspersed with fierce hand-to-hand fighting by ravenous hacks over choice morsels of approval dripping in honey from the *Irish Times* apiary. It's a nauseating affair but all over in 15 minutes. After that the bloated figures, some of the best-known names in Irish journalism, waddle back to their desks, hideously-inflated heads lolling over keyboards, grossly overblown reputations and gluttonous appetitites satisfied for another day, the whole place one vast grotesque pulsating suppurating carbuncle of pride.

The queue for the vomitorium is another story but I don't want to spoil your lunch.

IN THE RIGHT MODE FOR MUSIC

I saw where the composer Nicola LeFanu recently told a music recital audience that the first thing listeners should know about a piece of music was its length: they would then know whether to put themselves in the Webern mode or the Mahler mode.

She's dead right of course, and her insight applies to more than music. All sorts of things go terribly wrong when people forget to measure up properly and then find themselves in the wrong mode with no comeback and a bad headache at the end of the day.

Say you are in hospital for a sample, excuse me, I am slurring my words again, I mean in hospital for example. Right. Nothing too serious of course, minor medical mix-up, maybe you've got Bright's Disease and he's got yours, take just a few days to sort out. Anyway, a kindly vistor promises to bring you in some reading material, and you, your head swimming a little (just a gentle front crawl, one or two lengths, nothing strenuous), catch a mention of Warren Peace. Fine, you whisper gratefully, you look forward to making acquaintance with some light romantic writer (no more than ten stone two in his socks).

What happens? Your pal trips in next day and drops Tolstoy's greatest under-read novel of all time on top of you, both volumes, even in paperback the look of them is enough to set back your recovery by three weeks and the weight on your knee will do you no good either.

Sick or not it's your own fault, you should have asked the length straight off, confessed you were not in Tolstoyan mode, more Anita Brookner or Robert James Waller, max 120 pages, you'd be on your feet again in no time and taking a turn for the nurse ha ha.

But listen. Why should the mode-selection onus be on the audience? I mean at a concert? Why should you have to change your mode just because of what is on the musical menu? And say you are in foul humour, big row with the wife over your third glass of wine at the interval, would you be *able* to change your mode at short notice?

Surely any decent conductor should immediately be able to suss out the audience mode? Listen man, we are talking of *conductors*: men who make sense of orchestral scoring, who know how many keys French horns come in, that violas, all but the most finicky ones, play in the alto clef, that the English horn dissimulates shamelessly in sounding a fifth lower than it is written, that the tenor clef is used by bassoons and tenor trombones in those lofty volumes, the high registers, to save the poor copyist having to employ (at top union rates) too many ledger lines. Now do you really think such men will be fazed by mere mode analysis?

Say you are such a conductor. Take a good gawk at your audience. Do they look highly expressive and chromatically-inclined? Would they be up to some genuinely individual orchestration? Do they look like a crowd out for a good time, who won't kick up at an oul' bit of progressive tonality? A bit of Bohemianism in their make-up maybe? Would they stand up to some hard-eged contrapuntal clarity of instrumentation? Right. Hit them a good wallop of Mahler. Go on, warm them up with *Das Klagende Lied* and then what the hell, go for *Resurrection,* you have the right crowd for it if your mode analysis is on the ball.

Say on the other hand your audience looks a bit shifty. Some of the husbands have the look of men who would rather not be there, couldn't tell a governing tonal centre from a central toning governor. And yet, and yet – is it possible not all of them sport the Brunner or Synge Street profile? Yes! Here and there, dotted about the auditorium are a few who bear the unmistakeable Continental sophistication redolent of the 12-Tone Viennese School! Right. Out with the Webern, they won't know what hit them but it won't hit them for too long and that suits them. Sure everyone knows brevity is the soul of Webern, so go on, grab a few bits from the fellow's aphoristic period, get those legs going with the odd intervallic lep in the air, try *Kinderstück* or a bar or two of *Enflieht auf Leichten Kähnen* and you won't go far wrong, everyone out well before closing time, keep the orchestra happy too, all of them home on the last bus.

A WORD IN MR JACOBSON'S EAR

I see where Jewish writer and Joyce expert Howard Jacobson has been defending – no mention of the fee, I suppose it's standard senior counsel stuff plus the few bob for the junior – the anti-Irish joke, in the wake of the £6,000 - odd given to an Irishman in England who took a court case after he was forced to leave his job. "It is", says Mr Jacobson, "absolutely vital" that we should be able to tell jokes about one another, whether they be about Jews, mother-in-laws, women or Irish people.

Is is just me or does anyone else feel their limbs start to seize up on hearing something is not just vital but *absolutely* vital? Do you get the feeling you have urgent business to attend to elsewhere, does a peculiar giddiness overcome you, does your heart ache and a drowsy numbness pain your sense, do your eyes flit nervously about the room, looking for a, well, who can say, a refill maybe, or anyone you might talk to? You do? You do! Oh thank God for that, you don't know what this means to me, the feeling I am not alone, that someone understands.

The slightly worrying thing is that Mr Jacobson, a fellow with high seriousness dripping off him –

Like stalactites in the Ailwee Cave.

Quite. Normally I not interested in dreary literary devices such as similes, but let it pass.

Ah thanks.

Don't mention it. Now, as I was about to say, Mr Jacobson is currently working on a series of programmes about what makes people laugh. And (naturally enough) as someone who is (intimately) involved in the thigh-slapping rib-tickling gut-busting business (myself) you might (well) expect me to be deeply interested in his research, his findings, his interviews, the whole panoramic spread of his investigations, the nature of his philosophical-intellectual approach, and of course any oul' jokes he might come across.

But this is not as it happens the way I feel at all. It does not seem to have occurred to Mr Jacobson that he and his programmes may well place my employment in jeopardy. How does he think I am going to survive in this cut-throat every-man-for-himself business of "humour"if the secrets of my craft are laid bare and everyone gets in on the act, scintillating wit dripping off every Joe going the roads, the skilled cut and thrust of rapier-like verbal exchange and fabulous repartee soon available to any eejit that happens to view this series of programmes, the poor skeleton of my art laid bare for all to see? Does this fellow know (or care) how many mouths depend on my miserable but honest occupation? I doubt it.

Ah, I'm not all that worried. Many's the brainy lad before him that looked for the secret of giving people a good belly-laugh and fell on his face at the first fence. For what is elemental in humour; what material makes up its essential core, what inscrutable qualities make up the elusive mosaic of wit, and what creates the reality of laughter, the laughter of reality, the seriousness of high comedy and the comedy of high seriousness is not going to be thrown up on your TV screen in 4x30 mins or whatever this fellow and his producer friends have in mind.

At least I hope not. If he does look like letting the rabbit out of the hat I'll be slapping him with the biggest injunction I can find, I have friends in Palmerston Road and routes south, people who matter, let him not think I am a walkover here.

I read also where Mr Jacobson "can't bear to see the word abused".

Well (allIcansayis) he better keep his sensitive nose out of this column because as far as I'm concerned a vocabulary is only good for one thing and that's hard work. And mollycoddling words is not my line at all, when I round up the 750 or so I need I give them a good talking to, tell them exactly what I want, get them into order as fast as I can (the stint in the FCA did me no harm at all when I went for this job) and take no nonsense whatsoever from them, the slightest bit of cheek or smart answer or any hint of tomfoolery and I just lather into them with a good strong sally rod, any impertinence after that and they're out on their ear and that's the end of it.

OF ENERGY, WATER AND THE DANCE OF LIFE

I see where the eminent playwright Frank McBeamish – no, no, I have him mixed up with the Cork cousins, I mean Frank McGuinness, enthusing about J, em – Synge (and did you like our uplifting headline on the report: "Synge's brave vision inspires playwright's battle against laryngitis"? A marvel of medico-bellicose precision).

Anyway, Frank is keen on Synge's characters, who "dance on the still, sad music of Wordsworth's humanity and create instead a harshness, at times a frenzy of energy, a dance of life, life lived energetically at the very edges of humanity."

But, but (shakes head slowly from side to side, creases forehead fiercely, assumes expression of complete non-understanding, but desperate wish to know, genuine all-out *faux-naíf* child-like bafflement) – why distill sad music (of Hugh Manity, how they miss him in Doolin, Ballyferriter, Castlegregory, anywhere good music is appreciated) at all, surely that's only squeezing all the goodness out of it.

Yes indeed, a frenzy of energy, a dance of life, hold on here, I need a drink of water, the heat is fierce, these radio Riverdance re-runs by the Wey have me wore out).

What I am about here this morning is creating a conjunction – water, dance, energy, life as it should be lived, energy and no slacking. Take a gawk at the following:

"No one objects to a bit of detached, arty 'auteurism' between friends of the French New Wave".

No, no, not at all, why would they, go on Tristan (Davies, in the *Daily Telegraph*, reviewing videofilm):

"– but the first offerings in this collection show why Claude Chabrol's name ranks behind those of contemporaries Rohmer, Truffaut and Godard."

Auteur auteur, beg pardon, slurring again, I mean oh dear oh dear, fourth place in the race isn't bad in my book but I suppose if it's fourth and last that's another story.

Anyway. "Audran stars too in *Les Biches* (*The Does*) (What would be French for *The Dont's* I wonder) as Frédérique, a rich, beautiful, bored bisexual who lures a young girl painter Why (And Why not, you might well ask, if you only knew Why, as played by Jacqueline Sassard) to her villa in St Tropez for sapphic self-discovery. Fred shares her villa with two male slatterns who grow jealous, but it is Jean-Louis Trintignant's architect Paul who completes the *ménage á trois*, first by seducing Why, then being seduced by Frédérique."

Yes. Do you ever get the feeling you're not living at all? That life is passing you by, that on the rich tapestry of human experience you are only an undifferentiated speck, you are not making the most of your opportunities, your God-given talent?

Speaking of opportunity, I see where a US firm has applied to Galway County Council to buy 10 million gallons a day of Lough Corrib water for export in bulk tankers to Middle East. Never mind the investment and job potential here, I am concerned about spiritual depletion. After all, one of my colleagues, writing about this venture, has pointed out that we are ourselves mostly water (or in his case, Waters).

Hold on. What about our soccer team, and all the water they have swallowed on the hot pitches of the US? Does this mean they have been creating more of themselves? Is it possible that, depending on water intake, we have at times had more than the quota of 11 players on the pitch? Yes. But keep it quiet.

Don't forget about (the sands of) time running out too. But we are into extra time tonight, because July is late this year, and without excuses either, shameless unpunctuality. And this being the last day of June, scientists are adding a second to Universal Time at midnight. Hard for them to be working that time of night but they have no choice it seems, they have to correct an infinitesimal slowing of the earth's rotation, which has caused solar time to get out of line with very accurate atomic clocks.

So don't be wasting that extra time. It's only terrible the way some people live only half their lives, lookit poor Kevin Barry a case in point, just a lad of 18 summers, ah well he never had to suffer the bitter Irish cold from November to March anyway is one way of looking at it I suppose.

HOME, HOME AND DERANGED

Good morning.

How'rye! So tell us: readin anthin interestin these days?

Yes.

It's very hard to find anthin worth readin at all these days.

Indeed. I have been given Garrison Keillor's story collection, *The Book of Guys.*

Who gave you that?

A gal.

Ah-ha.

If by that you are suggesting the gift was ironic, meant to convey some subtle message regarding my masculinity, my membership and standing in the male community, my habits, my hobbies, my relationship *vis-á-vis* herself and all her sex, I believe not.

I said nothin. So is it any use?

It is some use.

Tell us the interestin bits then, leave out the rest.

The best story is that of Lonesome Shorty.

A cowboy! Ah I love a good Western story, very hard to beat the Wild West for adventure.

Lonesome is an unhappy cowboy.

What?

He misses the company of his fellow man, feels that animals, especially buffalo, do not make for a home, on the range or anywhere else.

It's a terrible thing to feel you're in the wrong walk of life.

True.

So what does poor Lonesome do?

Leaves the range, rides to Pit City and falls in love with Leonora, a beautiful redhead who, when not working at the Lazy Dollar Saloon, does Lonesome's laundry and cradles her head on his lap in a bower of prairie grass.

No shootin then.

Not a lot.

That's not my idea of a Western, I like six-guns blazin, saloon swing doors pushed open kinda slow, guys gettin shot plumb through the heart, lots of fellers a'drinkin and a'whoopin and a'hollerin an smoke risin lazily from the barrel of a Colt 45.

Quite. Lonesome becomes restless, feels he is still a cowboy at heart and must be out on the range.

Good man!

The relationship with Leonora becomes troubled, he clams up, refuses to talk.

Women hate that. What does she do?

Explains to him that silence is a form of anger, that a person can be just as aggressive with silence as with a gun.

I'd say Lonesome doesn't react well to that.

He goes to the saloon and gets extremely drunk.

There's many a person would blame him there but not me. What happens then?

Leonora explains to Lonesome, when he sobers up, that they are in a dysfunctional relationship, that Lonesome is a man who avoids conflict, that male restlessness, as evidenced by him, may result from a hormone imbalance caused by an eating disorder.

I don't like the sound of this at all, I think I know the way things are headin.

Lonesome agrees to go into therapy.

I knew it.

The therapist suggests to Lonesome, through the medium of a cat, that riding the open range is his way of repressing memories of his late mother.

Lonesome doesn't go for that I'll bet.

He tells his therapist that her analysis, and you must pardon me here but I am merely quoting Lonesome, is "the biggest crock of horse poop" he has ever heard.

Good on him. What then?

He rides outa town, beg pardon, out of town, but eventually comes back to Leonora, settles to a job at the stagecoach office as assistant director of customer service and group sales, cracks up shortly afterwards, robs a bank, rides off to the big mesas, dies of a fever, is eaten by vultures and goes to Heaven.

That's it?

Not quite. He gets fed up with an angel who sings beautifully but always the same song, and starts making plans to do something bad enough to get himself sent to the other place. Being a cowboy, he reckons, sorry, imagines, this will not be a problem.

Listen: this gal who gave you The Book of Guys, are you sure she meant nothin by it?

Reasonably.

TENSION, THEOLOGY AND CINDY CRAWFORD

I see where a college lecturer, Ms Louise Gilligan, has been urging us to "find ways of articulating an embodied theology which moves beyond the false and meaningless divisions of our medieval past – which divide body and soul, earth and heaven. This theology would interweave an appreciation of sensuality and sexuality with spirituality and sacramentality."

She's right, it's a hopeless business trying to articulate the oul theology thrown at us most of the time, with no body worth speaking of, no nor heart neither, and no household skills of old at all, useless at the simplest plain and purl, never mind interweaving appreciations of sensuality and sexuality and sew on.

But what am I "getting at", you ask?

Well ekshually, I (myself) have a major thesis (to present). And nothing will do me here but firstclass hons, *summa cum laude* stuff, top-of-the-class, gold medal, part-time tutoring to follow, then the statutory lectureship, professor's chair, on to the lecture circuit, interesting young blondetressed bluestockings hanging on my (every) word, Seamus Heaney eat-your-heart-out territory, the good life, international travel and seminars and Emer Eat Us Professorships, plus, with other likeminded geniuses, conversations of historic interest that will appear in literary magazines in years to come (as Marie has it).

My thesis? The nature of creative tension within an artistic duo, the relations of art to marital strife and the fierce rows that blaze up when two egos compete.

My raw material: Pierre Bonnard and his wife Marthe, Richard Gere and wife Cindy Crawford. Plus of course Scott and Zelda, the usual twosome at this table, the old reliables always ready to make up the numbers here with the Piat D'Or and the Bendicks (Joe and Yvonne).

Anyway. Take a good gawk at just about any Bonnard in the current Hayward Gallery, London show and you'll see a picture of domestic paradise. But what was the reality? Did you say "rather different, I imagine"? You're right. The wife, Marthe, is in nearly every picture. So did she spend all her time posing for Pierre then? No. She gave him just enough time for a few quick sketches and then the fellow had to work from memory in the studio, while Marthe did the dishes or whatever.

Though not dinner, according to Australian art critic Robert Hughes, who has described her as "a nagging, neurotic shrew who made life miserable for Bonnard and his friends, knew nothing about painting and could not even cook." Well *ekshually*, according to *mey* research, Marthe exhibited in Paris, where her work was admired by Monet, yes and by Monet another too, so there you are, Bob, put that in your barbie and smoke it.

But why, you ask intelligently, did Bonnard paint so many pictures of his wife in the bath? Because that's where he kept his artistic materials perhaps? Very funny. Because she spent so much time there. Poor Marthe was difficult, reclusive, agoraphobic, obsessed with keeping herself clean – but not the house. No. The housework suffered down there at Le Bosquet. And yet out of all this, Bonnard's great work! *A tidy home is no guarantee of lasting art.*

Meanwhile superstar Richard Gere is in the news for having spent four hours with "starlet" Uma Thurman over a Chinese dinner, giving rice to rumour regarding the state of his marriage. (Vermont, I think). And wife Cindy has told *Vanity Fair* that Richard does not regard her modelling career as highly as his own acting: "I don't know if he understands it or gives it as much weight as his career."

I don't know either. Is there *anyone* out there who "understands" a modelling career? Or any genius who ever gave the wife as much "weight" as his own career? I doubt it very much. In the world of creativity, fair play and understanding and sometimes even common politeness go straight out the window, very sad of course in human terms, but that's the price of art.

Listen, Scott, open another bottle of red there, where would I be without yourself and Zelda to give the whole thing balance, the two of you went through this mill many's the time, whenever I want advice on the subject it's youse I turn to, sure you know that well. Fill up those glasses, the night is young.

STANDING UP FOR THE LIBERAL AGENDA

I see where my colleague Nuala has been defending us journalists against charges of promoting the "liberal agenda."

The "liberal agenda" indeed. Who does it think it is showing off the fancy quotation marks everywhere it goes? Wouldn't it make you laff the way an oul jumped-up phrase probably from peasant farming stock no better than its neighbours gets a hold of a pair of inverted commas and won't let go for lover money?

Anyway. Nuala has been pouring scorn, out of the newsroom bucket provided for that very purpose, on suggestions that we are all out to push a godless society on decent Irish people.

Ah now it's not so clear. Take a look at last Monday's paper and maybe even today's, there's Nuala across there *on the left*, if you think that's an accident you're not as smart as I figured. And where is the voice of conservative Ireland? As represented in *Paper Round,* simple weekly round-up tales of luring the Eurovision Song Contest westwards, Blessed Virgin visitations, opposition to halting sites, worries over US tourism slump, nudist beach developments, all the stuff of grass roots Ireland? Where do we place these ordinary humble tales of placid country folk? Yes. Up there *on the right*.

Yes. And middle of the road stuff, prose and cons of the national situation, thoughtful modest special interest on the one hand/on the other hand/everyone entitled to their point of view but I'd just like to say one or two things if I may stuff down the middle, and finally a bit of a laff then if you're lucky, when you collapse with the strain of it all and tumble down here to the bottom of the page and run the risk of being charged with disturbing my piece.

Not very funny so far. I agree.

Anyway. Why shouldn't (sticks neck out, hands on hips, jaw jutting, eyes flashing dangerously) the "liberal agenda" be promoted? If we don't promote the poor crathur who will? Hold it back a year, is that what ye want? Is it to be left behind languishing in Ard Naonraí while the rest of its pals go on to Rang a hAon, poor "liberal agenda" left crying its eyes out repeating the year, simple addition and C-A-T (cat), subject of cruel sneers from former schoolmates, all kinds of childhood trauma to surface in years to come, career prospects maybe blighted for ever, unable to deal with ordinary social life or interpersonal relationships?

Easy, easy, we're all with you on this.

No I will NOT go easy, I DON'T CARE IF I'M SHOUTING, lack of promotion is a terrible thing, what about the poor crathur in years to come, stuck on the last-but-one rung of the Civil Serice, asst clerical officer grade 2, is that where ye want it?

Now hold on.

No! I'll not be silenced here, human rights are involved, a poor crathur that never did anyone any harm, still living at home, the mother's only support in her old age, turning to drink in his late twenties and what's before him then only long lonely years on the twenty-eight acres and dreams of what might have been, meeting Maureen or Gobnait in some sad ballroom of romance once weekly, having to be satisfied with a court on the way home and him fortyfive if a day, crying over the fireplace with the naggin of Paddy in the long nights after Samhain, deprived through no fault of his own of a happy home with children growing up in the sunlight.

Listen –

Shut up! I'll not be silenced when some poor dacent soul's life and happiness are at stake, let me say this now, I will promote "liberal agenda" for as long as I live, let ye make no mistake about that, I was never one to back off from the unpopular cause, no nor any of my people before me neither, we were always ready when the call came, not like many I could name.

What? God I would, thanks I'd love a cup of tea, yes, oh well just a drop for flavour, easy there, easy, you're a dacent man. God I'm sweatin.

CONVENIENCE FOOD FOR THOUGHT

There is much talk about a new book, The Marriage of Time and Convenience.

Sounds like a very odd match to me but there again you see some peculiar couples and they get on very well together.

True.

Would I like it do you think?

That may depend on how you read it. You are urged to read its 256 pages in exactly three hours because that is the span of the hero's life described.

I often find myself reading three books at the same time.

Have you some objection to reading at the speed of life?

Light travels at an awful rate, there's no way I could keep up.

I said the speed of life. But perhaps you are, as one reviewer has put it, the kind of reader who finds such authorial intervention a bit gimmicky?

No, no, I'm not averse to new ways.

You don't find it an unwelcome interruption of the *trompe l'oeil* we all crave in fiction?

Listen. Will you just tell us what it's all about?

It is a philosophically subversive study of time.

Sounds like heavy going.

Not necessarily. It simply tells the tale of Luke, a computer programmer run down by a bus but miraculously unharmed. The shock makes him realise some things are too big to see until they crash into you, literally or metaphorically.

It's hard to miss a bus all the same, you'd want to be fairly blind or else not concentrating at all.

Luke has decided to leave England for Italy and the three hours of the book cover the period prior to his flight.

I find no matter how much time you have before travelling somewhere you always end up rushed at the last minute, some people say it's better if you don't start preparing too early.

Such matters are actually addressed, though in a rather more sophisticated fashion, if you don't mind my saying so, in this book.

Is that right?

Yes. Inertia is considered as a very real factor, sometimes for example resulting in people's complete inability to carry out superficially simple tasks, such as getting to a particular place on time.

The train is the one thing I'm always inclined to miss, I don't know what it is but I always get there just by the skin of my teeth.

The book is leavened too with tips to help one survive life in the urban jungle.

You couldn't have too many of those. So what happens?

Luke's girl-friend Carmen "pops" a certain question related to the title of the book.

Ah-ha. I have you now, it's a romance, the whole thing, am I right?

After a fashion, perhaps. Carmen is, after another fashion one might say, the "big red bus" already mentioned.

On the heavy side, Carmen? A fine big agricultural Irish girl is she?

You are rather too literal. What I mean is that Carmen's attractions, while regularly in front of Luke, are not clearly seen by him *because* he is so close to her. It is like standing too close to a jumbo jet; you do not see the aeroplane as an aeroplane, all you see is a small expanse of metal.

If I was Carmen I wouldn't be too flattered being compared to buses and aeroplanes, and people being advised to stand back in order to get a proper look at her.

Carmen can stand up for herself.

I don't doubt it. But the whole thing sounds a lot too arty-smarty for my liking.

Then it is likely you will not enjoy the book's occasional Sartrian trope.

What's that when it's at home?

One example occurs when the act of facing backwards in a car is likened to putting one's back to the future.

As long as it's not the driver I wouldn't mind. If it was him I wouldn't put much faith in the future.

The writer also suggests playfully that the way we organise our lives in terms of time is not at all unlike the arrangement on the printed page, with paragraphs of different lengths, the occasional exclamation mark and other emphases sometimes planned, sometimes chosen in haphazard fashion.

I like a well-written essay meself but it's not something you see very often these days.

LIVING, BY EXTENSION, IN THE ATTIC

Eccentrics,is it? Don't be talking, man. I have been reading a newspaper plea written by a woman in England whose husband, 53, has retired to the attic.

Nothing odd about that you might say.

Hold on. How would I know what you might say? What gives me this unique insight into your possible reaction to any given remark of mine? Have I the slightest idea of how your mind works, how you might formulate responses, considered or otherwise? What makes me think, write, print such patronising remarks? Nothing but thoughtlessness, and I apologise.

Anyway. This fellow, now 53, retired to his attic five years back. Lately qualified as a teacher, he couldn't get work. He has told his wife that having worked since 16, his debt to society is paid, and he intends never to work again.

So what does he do with his time? He attends a BA Art History course (free, as he is unemployed), paints in the attic, uses his computer (for what is unclear). Occasionally he comes back downstairs to watch TV. He does his own washing and hangs it up (in the attic).

Well, you say, what's the problem?

Ah listen, sorry, there I go again, putting remarks, even questions, in your mouth, taking oral liberties I should be, indeed am, ashamed of.

But if you *were* interested, and of course I have no reason to think why you might be, the "problem" from the wife's point of view is as follows. The "Fat Man in the Attic", as their son has dubbed him, won't do any house maintenance, makes "menacing" gestures, has put on weight, won't diet, go for walks or see friends, except one couple. The wife admits she doesn't know "any more" just how odd his behaviour is, but it seems "damned odd" to her. She tells how she once suggested to him that he see a doctor, and he replied: "You're the one who needs a bloody doctor".

In conclusion she asks if there are "other 53-year-old men out there behaving like this to their wives".

As many as think they might get away with it, you might well imagine.

There I go again. Obviously I have no control over this, there's hardly much point in even saying sorry, it's sheer habit and I'll just have to get treatment, but believe me, I don't mean it, I make no pretence of being privy to your imaginings.

But look. Note how the woman asks if there are other men out there behaving like this *to their wives*. (My italics, or the newspaper's, if we are being particular, and we are rarely anything else).

Let me say something very simply (shakes head sadly, removes glasses, cleans them slowly with spotless handkerchief, replaces them, drums fingers on desk-top, leans back and sighs deeply).

The man is not behaving like this *to his wife*. (Instantly becomes brisk, rises to full height, strides to blackboard, begins making rapid notes, speaks firmly and authoritatively).

The man is not behaving "like this" *to anybody*.

His behaviour is abnormal only from the viewpoint of a *supposedly* normal society, here represented by his wife.

This man is occupying himself mentally.

He is demonstrating his self-sufficiency in so far as he can.

What other gripes has his wife, you, no, I, ask? (I am getting this under control now).

He will not move house.

He will not buy life assurance ("I'm not going to be worth more to someone dead than I am alive").

He keeps the attic door locked at all times, even when he goes to the toilet.

I suppose that's enough to be going on with, you might well say. (A habit is a hard thing to break).

But is all this funny? Is it a riot, a scream, a hilarious example of domestic chaos, marital disharmony, family mayhem, tied up with personal idiosyncracy in a crazy world? It is, but only if you subscribe to the theory of the universe as a vast impenetrable mystery, worthy of nothing (in the face of chaos, ruin, destruction and misery) but brave joyous laughter (oh well and maybe a pint or two at weekends). Otherwise I suppose it's sad enough, so let's stick to formula one, many's the wise man chose it after long consideration of the other options.

RETIRE NOW AND TEACH LATER

I see where my colleague Kevin Myers has been commenting none too favourably on teachers' holiday arrangements, and on the proposal by ASTI that teachers should be allowed retire at the age of 50.

If you think I am getting into (or even INTO) this controversy you are very much mistaken (winks to acknowledge cuteness).

But the first thing is some research. Hold on till I get my "Education" file out. Right, here it is. Look at this. One teacher told the last ASTI conference he was incensed, insulted and gobsmacked (surely room for some saving in passive verb usage?) about criteria for early retirement, which have to do with admitting/proving incompetency: Mr Louis O'Flaherty cannily pointed out that "if you can prove your incompetency, you must be shrewd, not incompetent".

There is clearly nothing incompetent, and everything shrewd, about Mr. O'Flaherty. He goes up in my estimation also for not once mentioning Catch 22.

Anyway. Here is my suggestion. Instead of teachers finishing their careers early, would it not be better for them to start late?

I am aware this is not a new idea. What then is it, perhaps? Yes: an idea whose time has come.

But how will it work, you ask, all agog.

Here's how. Say you are a young fellow in proud possession of "the call", mad to get up from Mayo to St Pat's, tales of the Cat and Cage and other Drumcondra attractions driving you wild with excitement, and O'Connell Street by all accounts only a bus-ride away. Right. The big day comes. Off you go, entire village out to say a fond farewell, mother crying shamelessly, father with his firm handclasp and a few words of good advice (*Ne'er a borrower or a lender be*, or maybe *to thine own self be true*, something sound along those lines), younger siblings pushing shyly forward to share in the glory, then suddenly there is old John Joe Hartigan's hackney car, solid and dependable like himself, in you climb, the crowd parts, off you go to the station, waving once but not looking back. Jim hears the one sniffle out of you but can be counted on to keep quiet.

So your life as a trainee teacher begins. You are educated in today's up-to-the-minute psychological way, you learn about teacher-child "relationships", the discipline "procedures", rules on the employment and remuneration of substitutes, how to deal with "difficult" pupils (and parents) and so on, not forgetting, I hope, the passing on of the three Rs. Then at

22/23, you graduate. But do you start teaching? You do not. Without one day in the classroom, you go out on full pension for 50 years!

It is entirely up to yourself how you spend these years, on your (starting) salary of perhaps 20 thou p.a. There will be a temptation to go wild, of course. Your character and vocation will be severely tested. The first few years will be critical.

How would I myself advise you, you shyly ask? Live life to the full. You should travel, meet interesting people (avoiding bores is a job in itself of course), perhaps enjoy a few bittersweet affairs (don't go in for those love-hate relationships, they're a terrible nuisance, very draining), become expert in some obscure culture, and remember your health is your wealth. Watch out for drink and the wrong class of person.

The onus is on you not to go mad entirely of course. If you drop dead before starting (or finishing) the job, the Department can claim against your estate.

In your early seventies you begin your career "proper". For the Department to get their investment back you will have to teach for at least 15 years. (I am not going to see the Department done out of money in this, they will get value or I wash my hands of the whole shebang).

But what if, on entering the schoolroom, you are already broken down by the usual sad factors, drink and the like? Look on the bright side. You are a graduate not just of St Pat's, but of the school of hard knocks. Instead of being taught by a naive young thing still wet behind the ears, and elsewhere, your fortunate students have the benefit of a teacher who has seen a bit of life and the greater world.

It is a far-reaching scheme of course, requiring courage and vision. And those who kneel to the false god "economy" will have little time for it. The old mould has to be broken first. Willie Yeats put it well, God bless him, nothing can be sole or whole that has not been rent.

HARD TO FIND AN INACTIVITY HOLIDAY

I see where our columnist Y has been asking (and Y shouldn't he) questions about the sort of tourists Ireland attracts. Are there any, he wants to know, who don't want to be instructed in anything? Who just want to stroll along Atlantic beaches? Who hate golf and are not interested in tramping around castles while audio-visuals boom at them? Who may enjoy the life of the pub at night?

Just when Y has used up his daily interrogation mark allowance he answers these questions, which you thought were rhetorical, himself. The country does get such tourists – but the trouble is most of them don't have much money to spend.

They're not much use to us so.

Hold on. Scenario coming up.

Certainly sir we have a very wide range of holidays I'm sure you'll find something to suit well this particular holiday right here on special offer includes tennis lessons with a pro at 6.00 am each morning followed by windsurfing after breakfast and rock-climbing in the afternoon with deep-sea diving in the evening oh yes we insist on full participation we like our clients to get the best out of these holidays of course if you prefer you can take the canoeing course that's combined with pre-lunch abseiling plus whitewater rafting and watercolour class also there's markmanship oh yes perfectly safe you can include it in the module with flower-arranging to professional levels I'm sorry sir if I misunderstood you said what kind of holiday? No I'm very sorry we don't do inactivity holidays no I can't recommend anywhere that might goodbye to you too.

That's the way things are going in the holiday world. No lazy people may apply. Lazy people usually have no money and if you're rich you didn't get rich by strolling on Atlantic beaches in your "free" time.

But the big market is in the culture/heritage seekers. Now say your own little hamlet has benefitted very little from tourism, the only visitors are looking for directions somewhere else, so how are you going to make it "marketable"?

You have to set up a "story-line", and Bord Failte sets out five overall themes: The Live Landscape, Making a Living, Saints and Religion, Building a Nation, and The Spirit of Ireland. The storylines which might, well, evolve, within these themes could be Working with the Sea, Farming Through the Ages, Emigration and Famine.

Hold on. Another scenario. The community (bingo) hall, a townland centre, the Midlands.

Lads, lads, ah come on now, order, order!

Voice from the hall: I'll not be silenced! The Live Landscape with sub-theme Emigration and Famine is your only man, Jarlath Mongey's notion is the stupidest oul codology I ever heard, in the name of God is Mongey seriously telling us we'll draw the French and Eyetalian crowd here with Building a Nation sub-theme Farming through the Ages –

Shut up you pup, McCarthy, ye know nothing about it, your people wouldn't be up to building a cowshed never mind a nation, where were your crowd when the call came and the Mongeys were out there follyin' the flag? Ye didn't suffer too much during the Famine itself either is what I heard, ye still have a taste for a nice bowl of soup I believe?

(Laughter).

Mongey, you're nothing but a low cur, you and your people were always the same, the only culture ye ever knew was mushroom compost and maybe the poor cut of silage if ye were lucky.

You and your storyline notions McCarthy, the best storyline you ever came out with was up in court and you on the charge of rustling Mary Colleran's five fat heifers, if the judge believed you he was the only one who did –

Let me at him! Let go of me, I'll tear ye limb from limb, Mongey!

Yes. It's just I don't really have (shifts uneasily) all that much faith in village democracy. Though (of course) I am all out for culture, heritage, history, the spirit of Ireland, the living landscape, saints and religion, the folk memory of the famine, the building of a nation, the encouragement of farming, the proper appreciation of our maritime resources, the occasional pint of plain and the life of the world to come.

HE'S NOT THE HORSE YOU THOUGHT HE WAS

I was reading a short story by Muriel Spark a while ago about a man and a woman who regularly share a lift in a huge office block, wherein they wonder about each other's marital status, guess at each other's occupation, imagine how each lives, and fantasise about a possible relationship. In the end they meet, have dinner together, and appear to get on quite well.

But surely, you ask, rather breathlessly, there is more to it? Are they young people, do they fall madly in love, is there an affair, is it all over in no time, where are they from, do they have good solid jobs with a future and is there any hope they'll settle down, marriage with children, a nice house and a Toyota and a Continental holiday every summer?

You are of course making demands which the short story format is not designed to fulfill (and you display embarrasingly bourgeois concerns). However, if you will simply replace your tongue within your mouth I shall tell you. They are both young, Michael is in marine insurance, Doreen is a literary agent's assistant, they hit it off rather well on their first date and there is an indication that they may have a long-term relationship.

But what gives the thing its (Muriel) spark(le) is a little appended philosophy. "...The curious thing is", the author concludes, "that all the notions and possibilities that have gone through their minds for the past five weeks or more are totally forgotten by both of them. In the fullness of the plain real facts their speculations disappear into immaterial nothingness, never once to be remembered in the course of their future life together."

They are not the people they thought they were.

This is what I have been "getting at" here.

I am hugely interested in literature and the mind, particularly the business (and finance) of transference. The things that go on would amaze anyone. You may have seen where two Irish writers, Ms Rose Doyle and Ms Liz Ryan have each written, and almost simultaneously, romantic sagas whose plots and characters and language are incredibly alike. Hold on, I have a fancier way of putting that: *whose stories mirror each other in almost every detail.*

Isn't that amazing? The two books, *Kimbay* and *Blood Lines*, are set in the world of stud farms. It seem that even the fictional horses have the same background, inflections, conversations and romantic interests, ha ha. The two authors-to-be – I mean author(esse)s, have meanwhile been falling over each other (clumsiness not reflected in their work) to show publicly there are no hard feelings. They want to resolve this, Ms Doyle and Ms Ryan say it's all a msunderstanding, a msfortunate mstake a bshop could make.

Shocked voices have been raised of course: The paranormal! Literary zeitgeist! Sci-fi come true! But what is actually going on here? How did these characters seemingly replicate themselves? My own theory for what it's worth (go on, make a bid) is that the affair is an example of Capgras's Syndrome. What, you ask, intrigued? *What?*

(All right. Listen. Capgras's Syndrome is a disorder where sufferers believe that someone they know has been replaced by an identical impostor. The belief, usually treated by psychiatrists, is a delusional idea. A delusion in turn is defined as a belief that is held on inadequate grounds and is not affected by rational argument. It is not the belief itself that is usually a problem, but the degree of emotion with which it is held and the actions the patient takes to bring him/her into the remit of psychiatric care. Also the reasons given are usually too bizarre to be credible).

Right. The characters of one novel are real, the others are impostors because nobody can read two books at the same time *and there is no way the reader can tell which is which.*

Who then is the sufferer? Why, the reader, sucked into the vortex of either of the two sagas. It's sad but that's the way it is. (I need hardly add) there is no cure. The authors meanwhile are in the heartbreaking situation we so often read of in the tabloids, their offspring switched at birth, no way of knowing who is whose, it's a hard thing to say but they should have attached the tags straight off, it's too late now.

HAND ME DOWN A SECOND-HAND MISTRESS

Today's theme is that of so-called artistic exploitation, though I may also refer in passing to artistic licence, the demise of the life class, and, I'm not sure how to say this, the nature of – well, em, ah, er,oticism. I may also, if allowed by time and space – those saucy imponderables! – cast a fond and nostalgic eye on *Jugendstil*, primitive heterophony and the general carry-on of the poor old *fin de siécle* crowd, God love them. To get full value you will need to pay attention, so keep your seatbelts on until the light goes out, though if you cannot keep up with a conversational level which will make few allowances for educational gaps, you are probably better off staying at home where you are less likely to be embarrassed.

I suppose that rules out anyone under 30 bar only those smart enough to drop out of formal schooling early, ha ha.

Ha ha. If however you are handy enough with the old *bon mot* and the odd classical allusion, if you can supply without prompting the occasional apposite quote from Yeats or Catullus, and you can keep the side up in the drawing-room with the ladies after dinner by means a verse or two of some stirring ballad, and hold your drink without making a complete eejit of yourself, for we are all men of the world here yet aware of our limits, then welcome aboard and the stewardess will be along in a minute, it's all duty free.

No duty at all but to enjoy ourselves.

Please curb your excitement. Lunch by the way will be a highlight for those with any class of a cultured palate at all. I won't tell you now what's on the menu but the setting will have you amazed: we shall be dining al fresco at a sun-bleached wooden table made by a local carpenter (carpenter! The man's an artist) to resemble a piece of driftwood and balanced on a faux coral stone base, quite stunning. That's only for starters ha ha.

Right. Exploitation in the arts. David Hockney was giving out stink a while back in one of the papers. " 'As for exploiting models' – he snorts with contempt (you can snort without contempt but it's not the same thing at all, a complete waste of time in my experience) – 'you should exploit lots of things. You should exploit talent' "

Well said, Davey. Now. C'mere. Did you read in our own paper a while back about the essentially Viennese artist Gustav Klimt, and how his models often served also as his mistresses? (Not only that but) he reputedly sometimes passed them on to younger artists with whom he was friendly.

Are you shocked? Go on, admit it. Really, I would rather you did so than hide behind a screen of hypocrisy, pretend to a false sophistication while denying your innermost feelings and betraying your strict moral upbringing.

Yes? You *are* shocked. Fine. There is no need for you to feel embarrassed. These are your principles and you must stand by them openly, make your aged parents proud, think of Peter and of how he felt when the cock crowed.

So you view Klimt's carry-on as (the very worst form of) exploitation. But wait! Let me show you how wrong you are. I align myself, using a good metal ruler and abiding by the old, though much-mocked nowadays, tradition of draughtmanship, with Mr Hockney.

You are making a number of mistakes:

(a) That was then, this is now. In those days no one gave a damn.

(b) The model/mistresses were well rewarded, Klimt was famously generous, if you think it was easy for a girl to make a decent living in Vienna a 100 years back you are wrong, those women would laugh if they knew the way you feel about them, your sympathy is quite misplaced, they all had the life of Reilly, or Klimt anyway.

(c) He could easily have thrown them out when he was finished with them, instead he got them placed elsewhere, that's the mark of a decent employer in my book.

But look. The notion of a second-hand mistress appalls you? It's good enough for Egon Schiele but not for you, is that it? What about art itself, then, I suppose you wouldn't have a secondhand Picasso in the house for love, or Monet? Surely you are aware the value of these second-hand, third-hand, fifty-fifth hand works of art has soared as they have passed from owner to owner over the years? Where then is the exploitation, provided the art is cared for and loved? Does it not yet cast its incomparable spell? So it is with the artist's mistress, more attractive, still as mesmeric, as lovingly handed on. If I hear you mention the word exploitation again I'll have you barred, look at the state you have me in, this is no good for the blood pressure at my age.

Story of an Up and Down Relationship

I was reading a salutary tale told in one of the British papers the other day by a young woman who began an affair with her neighbour.

I didn't think you read the tabloids.

On the contrary, this came from the pages of The Guardian.

I wouldn't be bothered reading about affairs, they're two a penny these days.

Your market valuation is probably accurate.

And "relationships" are even cheaper. Go on, you might as well tell us anyway.

The woman lived in an apartment on the floor above the young man.

Very handy.

Yes. Though initially, they hardly met at all.

Not even on the stairs?

No. But they were "on friendly terms".

How could they be friendly without ever meeting?

Please do not tempt me into cynicism.

All right, I said nothing.

Their friendship at first went only so far as mutual cat-sitting.

I hate moggies. They had no other contact?

None apart from the exchange of occasional jokey notes about her leaky bath and his fondness for rock music.

Many's the affair that started with jokes, if you can have a good laugh with someone you're halfway there.

But where?

Never mind. So they eventually got together?

Yes.

Well how?

She was getting over a bereavement, he became briefly ill.

Death and the flu bring romance?

It seems a direct quote is needed. "We were both at a crossroads in our lives and it was this, as much as a fast-growing attraction, that fuelled our affair."

Crossroads can be tricky. It went grand for a while I suppose?

She became heavily involved, he less so. She enjoyed the "sheer teenage fun" in the situation, what with creeping downstairs early or late and listening for the music that signalled he was home.

It sounds perfect but I think I can see what's coming, that sort of set-up has its own problems.

Excuse me: there is an acceptable form of words appropriate to the situation.

Tell us.

The very factors that had been fun at the start began to work against them.

Nicely put.

Yes. The sheer convenience of living so close together became tedious and the lack of formal boundaries became a trial.

I knew it.

Pardon?

It was getting more like a marriage than an affair.

You appear to have some experience in the matter.

What about your man? He felt trapped, did he? Am I right?

Please show some restraint.

Don't tell me: there is an acceptable form of words appropriate to the situation.

There is.

Tell us. In time, he felt oppressed by the lack of saving distance.

He felt trapped.

The crisis came toward the end of this one-year affair when the young woman spent a tortured night, aware that he had not returned home.

All over then bar the shouting.

And the real anguish, at least for the woman. After they broke up, the closeness of adjoining ceilings, walls and floors became a nightmare.

Hold on. I have an acceptable form of words appropriate to the situation.

Yes?

She found herself an unwilling auditor to his life without her.

Precisely. It was agonising for her to hear his phone ring late at night, to hear a female voice in his rooms, and laughter.

She moved out?

To a sympathetic friend's flat.

The poor woman. Did she learn something from the experience?

That if such a thing as a lighthearted affair really exists, it cannot thrive under such pressure-cooker conditions.

Fair enough.

THE CRISIS OF HISTORY, THE HISTORY OF CRISIS

According to a new book by three American historians (all women, though why I have put this in brackets I don't even know myself, it is almost certainly suspect) there is a major crisis in the intellectual life of the US, and indeed of the Western world. So what is it, you ask urgently, everything seems so normal, the sun is out now and then, your job seems secure, the cat is making a good recovery, what can the matter be ?

It is a crisis which apparently affects in particular the writing and reception of history: what is at issue is *the possibility of objective knowledge of any kind.*

Of course this is nothing new. The old positivism is well out the window by now. You don't need me to explain this to you, any decent post-modernist going the road knows the score, capitalism as useless as Marxism, nothing behind any of these tired ideologies but the desire to keep people down in the name of science and truth, the textbooks all racist, sexist and homophobic, all history, literature, science and religion long exposed as mere camouflage for the power exercised by white male capitalist elites, all ways of life equally valid, truth relative to the context, and the whole damn thing trapped in that old prisonhouse of language.

Isn't is a dreary old faith(lessness) when you think about it, sure what's the use of being an intellectual at all if there's no crack and nothing but disillusionment and flat pints?

No. We can't be going down that path, we want something better, something life-affirming, positive, uplifting, joyful, without of course going mad altogether for drink and women and late nights, that's the road to ruin.

What to do then? Attitude will be all-important. We must gird the intellectual loins, screw our courage to the sticking point, hold hands together and keep that lamp out of the water at all costs. There is a way forward, if not out of here, and we must find it.

The three authors of *Telling the Truth About History* (Joyce Appleby, Lynn Hung and Margaret Jacob, in parentheses once more I'm sorry to say) accept that history will never be the same again, and how would it be after the battering it has got? Yet despite everything, they nevertheless think it is possible to establish some correspondence between the past and the historian's account of it.

Do you feel happy about this? Does it not seem like hopelessly confused optimism? I cannot feel so sanguine. And I am intrigued by a review of the book by Sir Keith Thomas, in which he too reassuringly asserts that it is

"not difficult to discriminate between competing accounts of past reality".
Right, let's see about that.

Take a simple situation. Ask any two people about what went on in their home yesterday and the chances you will get two quite different accounts, even from the cleverer post-modernists. Say you had a row – and history is mostly rows of course. Forget the embarrassment, we are all adults here, could you repeat today word for word what passed between you and your spouse at the time? If you got the words right would you have the pauses, the inflections? Could you repeat the looks, could you make even a poor stab at recreating the whole angst-ridden stomach-churning gut-wrenching emotion of the thing?

Come on, you are an intelligent person, admit the task is beyond you, there is no shame in it.

What happened is history, what you write down now or tell me, is your account of it: one-sided, deliberately or innocently biased, leaving out essential elements, including and thereby over-emphasising the least relevant elements, you see you are back in that prison-house of words, voluntarily, when yesterday you were locked in there, you practically heard the door slam, it isn't the same experience at all.

Poor Sir Keith thinks that just because "the documents and material remains are there to be consulted and checked by fellow-historians, the experiment can be replicated and errors exposed." Oh yeah? Read history from the scribbled *billet-doux* and broken dinner-plates and thereby establish the truth of the affair (if there was one)? Ha.

I'm not at all sure that this is in the least funny, your complaints are understandable.

AND HOW IS YOUR BODILY-KINISTHETIC IQ?

I was interested in BP Fallon's remark in our Thursday Interview the other day: "The thing about education is that when you're learning to be cerebral and all of that, it's cool, but when they start messing with your head and trying to dilute and kill your instinct, it's crap."

There really isn't much more to be said, but still I think it is about time I got into the education "debate". I have been sitting on the fence for too long (damned uncomfortable it is too) and with about 25 years "formal" education under my belt (that accommodating cincture!), not counting the repeats or the "Finding the Boy I Was" weekends in Graingenamanagh and the Diploma in Masculinity Realignment (Maynooth), my point of view is surely as important as anyone else's, quite likely more so if I were to substitute honesty for modesty. Anyway I have numerous excellent points to make and if you can keep up with a style and content which may be rather demanding at times, you will learn much of value.

If space allows I shall be giving some career advice too on some of the more exotic "lifestyles" availabe to fortunate young people today, but will be steering away from the tedious business of points, "baffling" exam grades, the advisability of repeats, subject choice, single-sex schools, the stage in the family cycle when a parenting course is most advisable, and the ups and downs of Transition Year. Incidentally, anyone who subscribes (on an annual or even monthly basis) to those snobbish views on getting into "Med" will be well advised to stop reading now.

Turning first to the more cerebral aspects of education, I am greatly impressed with the work (as outlined in our very own *Education and Living*) of American educational psychologist Dr Howard Gardner, who has developed a theory of multiple intelligences, which challenges (yes, pistols at dawn, personal seconds, surgeon on standby, the lot) the notion that the human brain possesses one single intelligence that can by measured by IQ tests. If he's right it clearly means we will all need to be more specific when desribing someone as an eejit, a complete eejit or even a right eejit.

So far Dr Gardner has identified seven intelligences: linguistic, logical-mathematical, spatial, musical, bodily-kinisthetic, inter-personal and intra-personal. And having self-adminstered a variety of home-made tests (much cheaper than the branded jobs: you only need boric acid, a supply of Kleenex, a 5-ml measuring spoon, a drop of Jif, a four-foot rubber hose, a Bunsen burner and a little Worcestershire sauce) I found, despite my initial scepticism, the fellow seems to be on the right track! I discovered I have all these intelligences, most of them at a reasonable level, though it is a bad shock for me to have achieved only a very low score ("Sub-Average")in the bodily-kinisthetic area and worse still, and rather embarrassing to confess, "Near-Moronic" tallies in both inter and intra personal.

But why stop at *seven* intelligences? What about the spatio-temporal? The aesthetical, the anaesthetical and the synaesthetical? The annoying thing about people with pluralist theories (I find) is their lack of nerve, they just won't go for it, their caution would make you sick.

Anyway, Dr Garder would like the theory applied to education, with assessment specialists (a few jobs there) identifying what class of a genius every child is and "student curriculum brokers" (a few more jobs there) then guiding the kids to the most suitable subjects.

I see problems in this. Say your child (your beloved offspring!) is completely useless at almost everything but "Above-Average" in the "spatial" area. There he is going on 19, still at home, a big harmless lump *but great when it comes to putting together cardboard boxes.* What happens? Your student curriculum broker steers him towards architecture or engineering or at the very least gets him started as a line operative in Smurfits.

Right: say he finally qualifies as an architect, your joy knows no bounds, he is off your hands and set up at last. But. . .do you want a new civic office designed by someone (even your own son) whose linguistic intelligence is nil, whose musico-artistic IQ is so hopeless he can't even hum a bar of *Funiculí Funiculá?*

I don't think so. We shall have to fight this business, these radical theories. We want rounded people here, we can't have this at all. A firm line will have to be taken or we will make mistakes to haunt us forever.

Career guidance for the very confused

Nothing much doing today, so I will (take the opportunity to) catch up on some recent correspondence.

I have been remiss in responding to a letter writer asking for advice on the career of spin doctor, and politely expressing the hope that I am "free to comment."

I am always free to comment, that being one of the (few) perks of this job, but unfortunately can be of little help. Like many of my generation, I am rather tradition-bound in career matters, and have no idea what a spin doctor does, or how a person might get into the business.

This man goes on to ask if his daughter should marry a spin doctor.

Wait a minute. Hold it right there. Am I here to be handing out advice on who someone completely unknown to me should or should not marry? Would the girl even take her father's advice, never mind that of a complete, or even incomplete, stranger such as myself? Is it advisable for the girl to marry at all in these liberal times?

What kind of a girl is she anyway, fair or dark, tall or dumpy? How old is she? Can she cook a square meal or any shape of a meal at all, does she wear sensible clothes, does she take a drink or object to anyone who does? What sort of values does she hold dear?

Another thing. If I had any useful advice why should I give it out free, and people paying consultants good money? Would it be valued if it was given for nothing? Would it be easy come easy go? If I invoiced the man for 500 guineas wouldn't he be more impressed? Is he going to take amateur advice? On such an important business?

I would need to know the answers to all these questions and quite a few more before I would think of commenting.

The fellow is right however about such jobs not being advertised. My own belief is that those who get them are "head-hunted" by experts from the "human resources field." You read that because of continued expansion, unprecedented growth rate, enormous success, insatiable customer demand, unrivalled sales, huge diversification, dynamic client-driven market penetration, they need, excuse me, they are seeking to appoint, another "consultant." He or she will receive remuneration appropriate, in case you were thinking they might have the cheek to offer you something inappropriate.

By the way if you go for one of these jobs don't forget to "mark your application for the attention of" the named individual, in case someone else might get a peek at it and ruin everything.

There are some grand jobs going all the same if you knew how to get them. I saw a while back where a woman by the name of Lily Lodge was employed, and paid, as an etiquette consultant on the set of *The Age of Innocence*. What course would you go on for that job? How many points might you need? There is work here for a good careers guidance counsellor, I'd step in myself but I can't be doing everything.

And what about the fellow I told you about last May, Terence, the ethnobotanist and psychedelic philosopher, and doing very well too? Do you think his parents ever mentioned that particular career combination to him when he was a child, even in passing? I doubt it very much.

Look at your man Peter D Kramer, who made a mint with his book *Listening to Prozac* (the stuff which as you well know redirects the mood-enhancing brain chemical serotonin to the brain's frontal lobes and limbic system, where emotions come from). Do you know what Dr Kramer calls the people who deal in Prozac? Let me tell you: cosmetic psychopharmacologists.

You would be looking in Education and Living for many's the day before you would see that class of a job mentioned.

By the way it just me or does it seem to anyone else that there are jobs in every "field" except the agricultural?

Hold on. Who is the only man these days who is never referred to as being in a "field" (or even a particular field) of employment?

The farmer.

Who rarely if ever has to field questions (from the floor)?

The farmer.

Who among us is the only worker never to be heard calling for a level playing field?

The farmer.

Isn't that odd? It is very odd.

SANTA LAUGHS OFF SEASONAL RUMOURS

Christmas was coming again...

I saw recently where some psychologists were expressing reservations about Santa Claus being employed by parents as a threat rather than a promise: "Santa Claus is nice, we say, but he won't come if you're not nice. That is a horrible message to give. A lot of parents use Father Christmas, saying their children won't get any presents unless they are good." And so on.

I fell to wondering how Santa himself might feel about all this and decided there was only one way to find out. So after a long and extremely cold trip, I arrived at Santa's North Pole home, a modest detached two-storey igloo on its own 500,000-acre site.

I rang the bell and was heartily welcomed by Santa himself, an enormous roly-poly figure weighing about 20 stone and quite as jolly-looking as he is usually represented.

"Come in, come in!" he boomed. "Sit down, sit down!" he boomed. There was so much booming it sounded like a quarry-blasting. Santa knocked me merrily into a huge armchair and straight away handed me a huge tumbler of brandy and a plate of about 20 mince pies.

I was only half-way through explaining the purpose of my visit when Santa's wife, a gorgeous roly-poly little woman built to the same specifications as her husband but scaled down by a factor of ten, came in from the kitchen bearing a massive box of chocolates. I then realised to my horror that I had absent-mindedly consumed most of the brandy and all but one of the 20-odd mince pies; Mrs Claus took the remaining one away only at my insistence, clucking about the need to "build oneself up".

The Clauses themselves were so built-up that between them they could have passed for an inner city.

As we settled down over the chocolates, Santa told me he generally approved of adults ("they were children themselves once, after all") but explained, his eyes twinkling professionally, that "the distinction I make isn't between so-called bad and good children. It's between their *parents*. But let me show you."

So we went outside to Santa's workshop, where hundreds of happy elves were working away busily on teddies and train-sets and dolls, carols playing in the background and everywhere an atmosphere of great jollity.

Santa went over to the production line, took out the pieces of a toy wheelbarrow and invited me to assemble it. Maybe the brandy had something to do with it, but when I had finished, it looked like anything *but* a wheelbarrow. I think even the wheels were on upside down.

Santa was bellowing with laughter. "You see, that's the special model we deliver to *fathers* who haven't been as good as they might have been. Keeps them up all night. Wicked, isn't it? The ones that can be put together in three minutes, we deliver to any half-decent father. The same with lots of other toys. So now you know."

Well, I had to laugh myself. I suppose many a parent should have twigged this long ago.

We went on through the factory, Santa stopping regularly to chuck an elf under the chin, tickle another, merrily toss handfuls of them in the air and catch them again. The machines hummed, the elves sang, Santa laughed and I couldn't recall having had such a good time since I was a child myself.

Back in Santa's igloo, Mrs Claus had set the table with the most enormous dinner of turkey and ham. I presumed an army of famished guests was expected in at any moment from a 5,000-mile hike over the ice tundra, but to my horror found this mega-calorie meal was intended just for the three of us. What could I do but tuck in?

Over this gargantuan spread I told Santa all about the psychologists and their views and what they had to say about him and his symbolic nature and so on.

Well, Santa began to laugh. He absolutely howled, until Mrs Claus begged him to quieten down as Santa Junior ($2^1/_2$) had just been put to bed. Instead Santa laughed even louder and a moment later Mrs Claus herself had tears of hilarity running down her cheeks. The next thing I knew, Santa Junior, woken by the laughter, had come downstairs and was joining in the fun. A miniature version of his father, he rolled around the room in his holly-bedecked sleepsuit like a little Christmas pudding, emitting soprano shrieks of delight at regular intervals. His mum and dad occasionally picked him up and threw him to each other and the fun just went on until I thought the igloo roof would fall in.

Really, the Clauses are the most jolly people you could imagine. In the end, I realised Santa had never fully answered my questions. So I suppose I'll just have to go back again next year: with a bit of luck he won't answer them then either.

THE NIGHT AFTER CHRISTMAS

(With apologies to Clement C. Moore)

'Twas the night after Christmas when all through the house
Not a creature was stirring, not even a mouse
Silk stockings were still in their Brown Thomas pack
The wife planned (as usual) to take them right back
And exchange them for strong heavy-denier tights
A more sensible choice on these cold winter nights.
Myself I was nestled all snug in my bed
While credit card nightmares revolved in my head
With those seasonal greetings, so tender and sweet,
The most touching of all, "Did you keep the receipt?"
When out on the lawn there arose such a clatter
I sprang from my bed to see what was the matter.
"Relax", the wife muttered, "don't get so excited;
It's just one more party And you're not invited."
But the next thing I heard was a knock at the door
And when I went down there were neighbours galore.
They explained that their party had run out of beer
Which had quite spoiled the look of their seasonal cheer.
Their singing and dancing had lost all its rhythm
(And what drink that they had was all on them, not wythm).
So they wished me a loud "Happy Christmas to you"
and could I help out with a bottle or two?
Now I've found as a fact that wherever I roam
The virtue of charity begins in the home
And I just couldn't find the heart to refuse
So I brought them all in and broke out the booze.
They all cheered and insisted I wasn't the worst
For no fate could be crueller than dying of thirst.
Well we partied all night and we drank the house dry
After which we had breakfast, a huge Ulster fry
Then they all staggered off and I crawled up to bed
With the vaguest of notions as to where was my head.
So I took off my clothes then but only to find
That my legs and pyjamas were all misaligned.
As I foosthered and groped, the wife lifted her head –
"You're up very early this morning" she said.
There was nothing to do but put back on my clothes
And go downstairs again – where my blood duly froze

At the scene in the kitchen, the mess on the floor
Not to mention two neighbours asleep by the door!
Well, I gathered the bottles and cans in a sack
(and dropped Stanley and Joe in a skip out the back).
Then sneaked back upstairs but was trapped on the landing
For something had clicked in the wife's understanding
And she asked me a question that made my heart sink
(Well buoyed up though it was by an ocean of drink):
"You haven't forgotten, my sweet honey-bunch
That my mother and father are coming to lunch?
And you promised to cook that nice dish of roast pheasant
From the recipe list you got as my present?"
I could sense myself right on the edge of a row
The very last thing that I wanted just now
So I just had to do what a man's gotta do,
From the depths of a hangover serve cordon bleu.
If you ask me how lunch went, I'd have to say, well sir,
I winged it myself with a few Alkaseltzer
But there with the in-laws as I toyed with my plate
The last drops of my energy I felt dissipate
To keep my eyes open I just wasn't able
And I watched myself slipping right under the table.
Yet I managed to croak, as I slid out of sight –
"Happy Christmas to all, and to all a good night!"

BANK OFFERS RESOLUTIONARY NEW SERVICE

You'll be turning over a new leaf then?
Excuse me?
You know. The New Year. You made a few I suppose?
Pardon me?
For God's sake man. Resolutions. I suppose you have them all written down and numbered?
I am not keen on this business of making resolutions.
You're not?
No. You may be unaware that over half of all New Year resolutions are broken by the end of January.
My God. Is it that bad?
According to a number of surveys, it is. The same surveys suggest that only three per cent of people keep their New Year resolutions for a full year.
That's shocking altogether.
I quite agree.
I never realised it was such a hopeless business. But you're one of the three per cent then?
I'm afraid not. By the end of the year, however, I hope to have joined that exclusive club.
You do? How?
This year, I am having a set of resolutions made for me.
What?
Made for me. A unique new service.
Well that sounds like a great idea. Tell us. Is it expensive?
The personal package can be tailored to one's exact requirements.
Oh. That expensive.
I am assured the value is second to none.
Well it would be, wouldn't it, given that as you say it's unique?
Cynicism is unnecessary and unhelpful. Such a new and imaginative venture deserves better.
Ah well you know what I mean. But tell me: they'll make your resolutions for you. But will they keep them?
They will. Safe and secure, with full State guarantees.
Right. Now, say you give up smoking.
I am not a smoker, but you may use the example.
Okay. You give up smoking. . .
Excuse me. The NYRB gives it up on one's behalf.
The who?
The New Year Resolutions Bank, which provides the service.

Oh. Right. What happens next?

When my portfolio –

Your what?

When my portfolio of resolutions has been signed and witnessed, it is deposited in a sealed box in the NYRB.

That's all very well, but what about the nitty-gritty?

Pardon?

Keeping the damn things. Your resolutions.

I have explained that they are kept for me.

But dammit, what happens three days later when you stagger out of bed dying for a drag?

Why, if one must smoke, one must smoke.

But your resolution, man!

Entirely the NYRB's responsibility at this stage.

But –

Look here: do you use a bank yourself?

I have a few bob there. Why?

You write the odd cheque, make an occasional deposit or withdrawal and so on?

I do. Nothing major, of course.

And you have faith in your bank?

I do, I do.

Then surely you can trust the NYRB with a few rather ordinary resolutions?

Well I suppose so.

Good man.

You're quite sure my resolutions won't go astray?

The NYRB security measures are sophistication itself.

Well maybe I'll give it a go then.

You won't regret it.

Listen: would you have a drink?

I beg your pardon?

I said would we go and have a pint or two seeing the time of year that's in it?

As it happens, giving up drink is one of my New Year resolutions.

I thought you said the NYRB is keeping your resolutions for you?

I did and it is. I merely point out the fact.

Mulligans then?

Mulligans it is.